UNSOLVED
EAST ANGLIAN
MURDERS

TRUE CRIME FROM WHARNCLIFFE

Foul Deeds and Suspicious Deaths Series

Staffordshire and The Potteries
Colchester
Manchester
Guilford
Derby
Northampton
Pontefract and Castleford
Tees
Bedford
Bristol
Carlisle
Newcastle
Southend-on-Sea
Barnsley
Birmingham
Blackburn and Hyndburn
Chesterfield
Coventry
Ealing
Guernsey
Huddersfield
Leeds
Liverpool
Newport
Nottingham
Rotherham
London's East End
Wigan

More Foul Deeds Wakefield
Mansfield
Leicester
Stratford and South Warwickshire
Brighton
Folkestone and Dover
Oxfordshire
Black Country
Durham
Bradford
Cambridge
Halifax
Scunthorpe
Barking, Dagenham & Chadwell Heath
Bath
More Foul Deeds Birmingham
Bolton
More Foul Deeds Chesterfield
Croydon
Grimsby
Hampstead, Holborn and St Pancras
Hull
Lewisham and Deptford
London's West End
Norfolk
Portsmouth
Warwickshire
York

OTHER TRUE CRIME BOOKS FROM WHARNCLIFFE

Norfolk Mayhem and Murder
The A-Z of London Murders
Unsolved Murders in Victorian and
    Edwardian London
Unsolved Yorkshire Murders
A-Z Yorkshire Murder
Brighton Crime and Vice 1800-2000
Essex Murders

Executions & Hangings in Newcastle
    and Morpeth
Norwich Murders
Unsolved Norfolk Murders
Yorkshire's Murderous Women
Black Barnsley
Durham Executions
Strangeways Hanged

Please contact us via any of the methods below for more information
or a catalogue.

WHARNCLIFFE BOOKS
47 Church Street – Barnsley – South Yorkshire – S70 2AS
Tel: 01226 734555 – 734222 Fax: 01226 – 734438
E-mail: enquiries@pen-and-sword.co.uk
Website: www.wharncliffebooks.co.uk

Unsolved
EAST ANGLIAN MURDERS

Jonathan Sutherland and Diane Canwell

Editor
Brian Elliott

Wharncliffe Books

First published in Great Britain in 2007 by
Wharncliffe Local History
an imprint of
Pen & Sword Books Ltd
47 Church Street
Barnsley
South Yorkshire
S70 2AS

ISBN 978-1-84563-044-7

A CIP catalogue record for this book is available from
the British Library

Typeset in Plantin and ITC Benguiat by
Mousemat Design Limited

Printed and bound in England by CPI UK

Pen & Sword Books Ltd incorporates the Imprints of
Pen & Sword Aviation, Pen & Sword Maritime,
Pen & Sword Military, Wharncliffe Local History,
Pen and Sword Select, Pen and Sword Military Classics
and Leo Cooper.

For a complete list of Pen & Sword titles please contact
PEN & SWORD BOOKS LIMITED
47 Church Street, Barnsley, South Yorkshire,
S70 2AS, England
E-mail: enquiries@pen-and-sword.co.uk
Website: www.pen-and-sword.co.uk

Contents

Introduction

In writing any non-fiction book, the ultimate goal always has to be to give the facts in the clearest and most unequivocal manner. There is also the hope that information that comes to light after the book has been written does not undermine the research and the work carried out by the writers. This is not the case with a book such as this. In fact the authors would be delighted if the conclusions of the stories involving unsolved murders across the three counties of Norfolk, Suffolk and Essex, have a significant break-through after the book has been written and published.

Unsolved murders, whether they occurred a century or more ago, or just a matter of months prior to today, leave families in an invidious position. The unsolved nature of the cases leave so many questions unanswered and as time passes it becomes less and less likely that the cases will ever be solved.

The police, however, always and understandably take the view that an unsolved or an unresolved case will always remain open. In truth it is a matter of resources and priorities. We have seen in recent months the full resources of the Suffolk police, for example, supported by officers and expertise from out of the county, deployed to solve a present set of serial killings in the Ipswich area. Undoubtedly events such as this quite rightly take precedent over cases that relate to events often decades before.

Periodically the police will launch an initiative or a new appeal to try to jog the memories of residents in the hope that even the merest clue or piece of evidence can be unearthed. They know that it is often a forlorn hope and that with the best intentions and effort, as well as press and media coverage, they may not receive a single call to assist their enquiries.

In this book we look at cases ranging from the nineteenth century to the present day. We consider cases in Norfolk, such as the famous Susan Long case and the headless body of

Cockley Cley. From Suffolk there is the Peasenhall murder, still unsolved after 106 years, to more modern-day cases, such as the murder of Vicky Hall. From Essex there are the perplexing gangland execution-style killings, as well as the notable Red Barn murder. In the case of the latter, although William Corder was found guilty and was executed for the crime, there is a considerable body of evidence to suggest that he was innocent.

There are many instances of cases that have barely got off the ground. The police, unable to even identify the body, are left with a frustrating case with no lines of enquiry. Typical of these are the headless body of Cockley Cley and the unidentified body found in Dunston Woods. Other cases seem clear-cut, with a prime suspect identified very early in the case. But many of these have either led to sensational acquittals or serious miscarriages of justice.

All of the cases have unanswered questions. They are perplexing and sometimes very unjust. It is clear from many of them that the police, the media, neighbours and families only know part of the whole story and the truth. There are aspects of many of the victims' lives that have remained hidden for generations, or simply for months. Perhaps amongst these unknowns are the answers to why the victims were murdered and by whom.

In compiling these cases we have returned to original newspaper accounts of the investigations and, if relevant, the trials. By carefully looking at the day-by-day reports it is possible to piece together the activities of the investigating teams, to see where their lines of enquiry were and what motives and methods they were considering. Some of the cases are very well documented and have full trial transcripts, such as the bootlace murder in Great Yarmouth and William Gardiner's two trials for the murder of Rose Harsent.

However unlikely, perhaps there might be something in the re-examination of these cases to provide the reader with the merest clue as to the answer to some of these unsolved cases. The latest unsolved cases are either truly unsolved, despite the arrest and questioning of numerous suspects, or there is an individual tried and sentenced, but with the great likelihood that this person was unfortunately at the wrong place at the wrong time and that all efforts were focused on that person to secure a conviction.

Some of the cases will show the accused going through every bit as much pain and suffering as the victims' families, only to be acquitted of the charges that had been hanging over them for months.

We hope that we have chosen a representative selection of unsolved murder cases, covering almost 200 years. We have drawn from the archives of long gone local and regional newspapers. This has helped give a taste of the period and the feelings that were obviously running high in the regions whilst the cases were underway.

One major consideration to bear in mind is that some of the older cases would have been solved beyond any shadow of doubt if modern forensic techniques had been available at the time. The trace of blood on William Gardiner's penknife could have been identified as either that of Rose Harsent or a rabbit, as he had claimed. The precise cause of death of William Corder's alleged victim would have been established and CCTV footage would undoubtedly have been presented by the defence in the case of Bennett, who claimed to be in London at the time of his wife's murder in Great Yarmouth.

In presenting these cases we have only speculated once all of the facts, as they are known, have been presented. Our speculations merely suggest alternative solutions or answers to some of the most perplexing cases that have ever faced the police forces in the three counties. Our personal opinion has never entered into any of these cases. We leave that for the reader to infer and form their own opinions and solutions to each of the cases presented in this book.

Jon Sutherland and Diane Canwell
February 2007

CHAPTER 1

An Infamous Tale

The murder of Maria Marten, 18 May 1827

There was a private ceremony held in a Streatham crematorium in South London in August 2004. Distant relatives of William Corder had gathered to close one of the final chapters on a story that has intrigued thousands for several generations. The remains of William Corder, who had been hanged in 1828 for the murder of his lover, Maria Marten in the infamous Red Barn case, were finally laid to rest. His remains had been cremated a few days before. For three years Linda Nessworthy, whose grandmother, Laura Corder, was related to William, had been trying to get the skeleton of her ancestor released from the Hunterian Museum in London, which belonged to the Royal College of Surgeons. The skeleton had been in the museum since 1949. It was originally stored there under the Anatomy Act and Linda's success came after a decision made by the Working Party on Human Remains published findings, stating that artefacts such as the skeleton could not be held without the descendents' permission.

This was not the only part of William Corder to be placed in a museum for casual observers to peruse. After his hanging in August 1828 his body was dissected. It was cut open and laid out in the Bury St Edmunds Shire hall for hundreds to come and view. The surgeon, George Creed, dissected Corder's body. He removed the skin and then had it tanned to give grisly leather binding to an account of the murder and trial. This book and part of Corder's scalp are still in the Moyse's Hall Museum in Bury St Edmunds, but Linda Nessworthy also wants these back so that the final remains of her ancestor can be laid to rest. A spokesman for the museum said:

The whole Red Barn collection, including the account of the trial bound in Corder's skin and the part of his scalp, are artefacts of their time and help us understand how people thought about and dealt with crime and punishment two centuries ago.

These artefacts, together with a death mask in the museum, are only part of the continuing debate about the rights and wrongs of the trial and what became of Corder and parts of his body after his execution.

The Shire Hall in Bury St Edmunds.

In fact throughout his trial Corder maintained his innocence, but he was found guilty and it was said that seconds before sentence was carried out Corder actually confessed to the murder of Maria Marten, claiming that he had quarrelled with her about the burial of their child, amongst other things. A scuffle had then broken out and impulsively he had taken a pistol out of his jacket pocket and shot Maria. Whether this last minute confession ever took place is one of the key parts of the whole case that remains hotly contested.

It was indeed a major case at the time.

William Corder had been born in 1803 and was the son of a farmer. He lived in Polstead, near Stoke-by-Nayland in Suffolk. Over the space of eighteen months his father and three brothers all died. This left William and his mother to run their farm. Corder was only around 5 feet 4 inches tall and was nicknamed Foxy, whilst some others simply called him Bill. He had never got on particularly well with his father or brothers, but was very attached to his mother. He is described as being well muscled, with a fair complexion and freckles and, despite the fact that he was short-sighted, he was an excellent shot.

Corder was said to be rather reserved, but he loved gossip. He never drank to excess and the only money he seemed to spend was on women. On several occasions he had apparently obtained money by fraud. While his father was alive there was an attempt to send him away by getting him a job as part of a ship's company.

William was 23 in March 1826, when he became involved with Maria Marten. Maria already had rather close relationships with the Corder family. She had two illegitimate children, one of whom was the result of a relationship with William Corder's second eldest brother. She also had an affair with another local gentleman and her second child, Thomas Henry, had been born. The first child had already died and when she started her affair with William a third child was born, but died within the month. The pair of them took the strange pretence of taking the child to Sudbury for burial but they had, in fact, already buried the child in a field.

Sometime around this period William dishonestly cashed Thomas Henry's father's £5 cheque that he had sent to his son. On many occasions Corder promised to marry Maria, but always seemed to be able to squirm out of the final commitment.

Central to the eventual case was the Red Barn. It occupied

an isolated position on Barnfield Hill. This was about half a mile from Maria's cottage and a mile from Polstead church. Mrs Cooke of Polstead Hall owned the barn and the Corder family rented it, along with some nearby fields. They used it for threshing and storing the grain after the harvest. The barn was wooden with outbuildings and had an enclosed yard. At the time part of the roof was thatched. It was here that Corder and Maria often walked or met.

Some six weeks after the birth of Corder's child with Maria, therefore two weeks after it had died, Maria went missing. Corder was staying in Polstead and the Red Barn itself was firmly locked and the key in his possession.

Maria's family were understandably concerned as to the whereabouts of their daughter. Her father, Thomas Marten, was a mole catcher. He had several children by his first wife and after her death his second wife, Ann, bore him at least three additional children. Ann herself was only a few years older than Maria. The pair seemed to get on very well, but strangely it was through Ann Marten's dreams that the murder was finally discovered.

Rumour has it that Ann Marten may well have actually known about the murder. Some even suggest that she may have had something directly to do with it. The gossip was that she was romantically involved with Corder and that Maria was in the way. As some would later suggest, Ann Marten made up the stories of her dreams to try and ease her own guilty conscience.

As we have said, Corder was no stranger to the courts. On one occasion he asked an acquaintance of his father to lend him £10. Some time later, when William's father was asked by the acquaintance about the loan, he told him that he had no knowledge of it. According to rumour he had squandered the proceeds on loose women. On another occasion Corder's father sold some pigs to a man called Baalham. A few days later William sold the same man some more pigs. When William's father discovered that Baalham had more pigs than he thought he was entitled to he demanded their return. It was only then that the truth came out. William had been involved in several cheque frauds, presenting forged cheques to banks in Colchester and in Manningtree.

According to James Curtis, who wrote *The Mysterious Murder of Maria Marten*, which was published in 1828, Maria Marten was no real angel herself:

Possessed as she was of no ordinary personal advantages, consisting of a handsome face, a fine form and figure, and, moreover, a superior address, accompanied with a modest demeanour – for innocence and purity then lodged in her breast – with such advantages and attractions, it cannot excite much surprise that she should have been beset by admirers; nor, when we reflect upon what human nature is, does it appear remarkable that she, an artless inexperienced girl, should have listened to the voice of flattery, and been led to fix her more mature consideration and esteem. This was her unfortunate lot, and, in her eighteenth year, the heretofore happy and innocent Maria listened to the persuasions of the base destroyer, and became a victim to his cupidity, and lost that inestimable pearl – the richest treasure which a woman can possess – her virtue.

Curtis was, of course, referring to the relationship Maria had had with William's brother.

Meanwhile, we return to the point where the Marten family had discovered that Maria was no longer in the area. Several months had gone by and there was still no word. Corder was vague. At first he told them that she was staying with a Miss Rowland in Great Yarmouth.

On 18 October 1827 he wrote a letter to Thomas Marten from London, stating that he and Maria were husband and wife. He then told the family that Maria was staying on the Isle of Wight. The letter also stated that he was surprised that they had not written directly to Maria, because she had written them a letter, describing the marriage to them.

He also wrote a letter to Peter Matthews, who was the father of Maria's son Thomas. In the letter he explained that Maria had hurt her hand and could not write. When Matthews and the Martens exchanged correspondence they both became increasingly concerned.

For some time Ann Marten had been dreaming about Maria. She had had at least two dreams, one before and one shortly after Christmas. She begged her husband to search the Red Barn. In her dream she saw that Maria had been murdered and that she was buried in the Red Barn. She kept it all to herself for some time because she was afraid that her husband might consider her to be odd and superstitious. Now she was determined that her husband should investigate her premonition.

For some time he refused but then finally gave in to the

constant nagging. He took a friend with him to the barn and the pair of them began prodding the floor of the Red Barn with a mole spud. It is not clear how long this carried on for, but he eventually dug out some eighteen inches of loose earth and found a body stuffed into a sack.

Thomas Marten instantly recognized a green, silk handkerchief. It belonged to Corder and Maria was wearing it when she had left the house. They did not disturb the body but instead called the police.

A coroner, John Wayman, from Bury St Edmunds was summoned and, although it was a Sunday, he brought together a jury so that everyone could view the body. The inquest was held at the Cock Inn in Polstead. The identification was straightforward and a member of the family confirmed that it was Maria, from the missing tooth, the colour of her hair, the clothes she was wearing and the belongings found with her. It was clear from the outset that there was evidence that would implicate William Corder.

There was a good bit of detective work carried out by a local constable, by the name of Ayres. He obtained a contact address for Corder in London from his brother-in-law, who was a friend of Corder. Together with a London policeman, Constable Lea, they traced Corder and found him timing eggs for his breakfast. According to the *John Bull Magazine*, dated 27 April 1828:

He [Ayres] *arrived in town* [London] *on Monday having applied for assistance. The business was placed in the hands of Lea. With a loose clue afforded him by the country constable, he traced the prisoner first to Grays Inn terrace, and from thence through a number of intermediate places to his residence, in Ealing Lane, near Brentford, where he apprehended him. A degree of stratagem was necessary to obtain an entrance, and he procured it by representing that he had a daughter whom he was anxious to place under the care of his wife. On going in, he found him in the parlour with four ladies, at breakfast. He was in his dressing gown, and had a watch before him by which he was minuting the boiling of some eggs. Lea called him on one side and told him that he was a London police officer, and had to apprehend him on a most serious charge. He seemed somewhat alarmed, and at his request they retired into the drawing room, but on his being made acquainted with the nature of the offence, he denied all knowledge of it, as also of his unfortunate victim.*

Lea discovered a number of letters from a person called Gardner. He also found a case of pocket pistols, which were thought to have been purchased on the day of the murder, together with a powder flask and balls. It also appeared that Corder was going to leave the country, probably headed for France.

Amazingly, one of the women was Corder's wife. The report in the magazine went on to say:

> *A most respectable man* [Corder's brother-in-law] *having ascertained the serious offence with which he was accused, questioned his sister as to the length of time she had known the prisoner before she had married him. She answered, only for three weeks, and that she first became acquainted with him through the medium of a matrimonial advertisement, at a pastry cook's shop in Fleet Street, to which he had given a reference. She married him at the Church of St Andrew, Holborn in November last, and was quite unaware of his being guilty of any offence.*

Corder was packed off towards Colchester and at 2100 arrived at the George Inn. There was an enormous crowd waiting for him. Mr Smith, the landlord, managed to set aside a private and secure room where he could be kept. Lea left Corder in the custody of Ayres, while he went off to Colchester jail. The policeman was without a warrant so the jail refused Corder and, as a consequence, he was tied by one hand to the bedpost for the night.

During that night he wrote to his mother:

> *I scarcely dare presume to address you, having a full knowledge of the shame, disgrace, and I may truly add, a stain forever cast upon my friends, family, and late formed connections. I have but a few minutes to write, and being unfortunately labouring under this serious charge, I have to solicit that you will receive Mr Moore* [Corder's new brother-in-law] *on Friday morning, with whom may probably be my injured, lawful and I must do her justice to say, worthy and affectionate wife. I have always experienced from every branch of their family the kindest treatment – hope and trust the same will be returned from you the short time they continue in this part of the country, which I am sorry to have to state is to hear the event of this dreadful catastrophe.*

*I am happy to hear you are tolerably well, considering the cir-
cumstances. I may, perhaps, be allowed an interview with you
in a day or two, but that is very uncertain.*

There was some debate whether Corder signed the letter 'must
beg to subscribe myself your affectionate son' or 'must beg to
subscribe myself your unfortunately though unworthy son'.
The last paragraph of the letter had been altered.

Corder was taken to Polstead and from there he was remanded
at a hearing to the county jail in Bury St Edmunds to await trial.
The assizes were to be held at the Shire Hall during August 1828
and Corder's trial was set to begin on Monday the 4th.

It was already very clear that the trial was going to attract an
enormous crowd. *The Times*, reporting on 21 July, said:

*So great is the anxiety to be present at his trial, the lodging
house and hotel keepers in Bury are already speaking of an
increase in their usual assize prices.*

As it was, there were vast crowds and the hearing was delayed
until Thursday, 7 August. It had been announced to much
chagrin on Wednesday evening that women would not be
admitted to view the trial.

At 0600 on the Thursday, hundreds, if not thousands of
people surrounded the court. It took half an hour for the judge,
Chief Baron Alexander and other court officials to struggle into
the building. It was a hot, sticky day and Corder appeared in a
new suit of clothes. During his period on remand he had grown
a beard. When asked to make a plea Corder firmly announced
that he was not guilty.

For those that had managed to struggle into the courtroom
there were to be some sensational exhibits on show, one of which
was a model of the Red Barn and the other was Maria's head.

There was no doubt that a murder had been committed. The
problem was that by the time the body had been found it was
difficult to say precisely how Maria Marten had been killed.
Back at the coroner's inquest held at the Cock Inn in Polstead,
the surgeon, John Lawton, had testified:

*I was present when the body was viewed by the gentlemen of
the jury, and made as minute an examination as I could. I first
took off some pieces of sack which covered it; the body was lying
upon its right side, with the head forced down upon the*

shoulder. There was coagulated blood upon the cheek, and there appeared to be blood upon the clothes and handkerchiefs. The green handkerchief round the neck had been pulled tight, so that a man's hand might be put between the knot and the fold, and under it there was the appearance of a wound from a sharp instrument, but that part was so decomposed, I can only say that it had that appearance. The internal bone of the orbit of the right eye was fractured, as if a pointed instrument had been thrust into it, and the bone dividing the nose was displaced; the brain was in such a fluid state, that I am unable to say whether it had sustained any injury or not. Such a stab as I have described might have penetrated the brain. I found no injury in any other part; but there were two small portions of bone in the throat, which might have passed thither from the nose or orbit of the eye. I think the handkerchief was pulled tight enough to have caused death; the neck of the deceased appeared very much compressed indeed. The sack had evidently been tied after the deceased had been put in head foremost.

The witness had later stated that a pistol ball had entered the neck through the jugular vein and had then proceeded to the eye on the opposite side of the head, which would probably have produced a fracture on the orbit.

There were some cuts in the clothing, which could have pointed towards a stabbing. In all probability these were actually caused by Maria's own father when he used the mole spud to investigate the floor of the Red Barn.

The bill of indictment produced nine counts to cover all possible causes. However Maria Marten had actually died, the indictments all charged William Corder with having perpetrated the crime.

Before the court Corder seemed cool, almost indifferent. The *Essex Herald* described him as:

Of middle height, of a fair and healthy complexion, large mouth, turn up nose, large eyes, which had a fixed and glazed aspect, and his features bore rather a smile than any other expression. For a few minutes he conversed with his solicitor, and then stood up erect and looked at the judge, and bowed in a very respectful manner.

The prosecution described both Corder's and Maria's background. Mention was made of their affair and William's promise of marriage. The court heard about the conversations that Corder had had with several people and how the letters had meant to allay any suspicion about the disappearance of Maria Marten. Ann Marten appeared as the prosecution's first witness. She explained about her stepdaughter's relationship with Corder, the number of times that he had visited their cottage and the birth and death of the baby. She also told the court that on the morning that Corder had claimed Maria had left for Ipswich she had said to him 'Oh, William, if you had but married Maria as I wished, all of this would have been settled'. Corder had replied 'Well I am going to Ipswich to marry her tomorrow morning'. Ann told the court that this reply had not convinced her, but that Corder had tried to reassure her:

> *Don't make yourself unhappy. She shall be my lawful wife before my return, or I will get her a place until such time as we can be married.*

At the time this was all Ann Marten had heard and over the next few months whenever she saw Corder he tried to reassure her.

The next two witnesses were Maria's father Tom and his younger daughter, Ann. Tom Marten said of the dreadful discovery in the Red Barn:

> *When I had poked with my mole spike about four inches, I found something come out with it like flesh. We* [he and two other men that returned to the barn later] *then took up a part of the earth until we came to the body. The legs were drawn up and the head bent down.*

Even Maria's younger brother, George, then aged 10, appeared before the court. George told the court that he had seen Corder leave with Maria on 18 May but had then seen Corder later that day:

> *On the day they left our house, I saw him again coming from the barn with a pickaxe on his shoulder. He was then going from the Red Barn homewards. I am quite sure he is the person I saw with the pickaxe.*

When John Lawton, the surgeon, gave evidence it was time for Maria's head to take centre stage:

> *I have the head here and produce it. This is the jaw, and there are two teeth gone.*

Throughout Corder seemed unaffected and at this point the proceedings were adjourned until the following morning.

There was an even bigger crowd the next day. John Nairn and Henry Chaplin, two surgeons, confirmed Maria's injuries. Her sister and stepmother gave positive identification of Maria's clothes. It was now time for the defence to begin.

Corder himself appeared first. His counsel, Mr Broderick, had advised his client not to speak and that he would say that provocation had been the defence and that he should enter a plea of manslaughter. Corder thought his best hope was to say that Maria Marten had committed suicide. Corder stood before the court, now nervous.

He rounded on the newspapers. He then admitted that by not mentioning his version of events until the trial he had caused himself problems. He told the court that Maria had returned to stay with him after she had supposedly left for Ipswich. It was she that had gained possession of a pair of pistols that were one of the exhibits in court. On their way to the Red Barn on 18 May there had been an argument. Corder said that Maria had flown into a rage while she was changing her dress. Instead of wanting to marry Corder in Ipswich, she wanted to go home. Corder left her and headed out of the barn. He had no sooner disappeared from sight when he heard a shot. He ran back in and saw Maria lying on the floor dead. He admitted that he had been wrong not to immediately say anything and then to bury Maria's body in the barn.

Corder asked the jury to believe that he would not have shot Maria and buried her when it was highly probable that her body would be easily found. In fact he pointed to the fact that he had stayed in Polstead for some time after the death. He had then headed for Portsmouth then the Isle of Wight and then married and moved to Brentford.

Witnesses supported the fact that Maria had access to the pistols. The rest of the witnesses simply attested to the fact that Corder was a good man. It was now time for Chief Baron Alexander's summing up.

It was a quiet and deliberate speech. The judge pointed to the fact that it was a subterfuge that Maria had actually left home. Corder had admitted that he had placed the body of Maria Marten in the Red Barn. The judge thought that the most damning part was the fact that Corder's suggestion that Maria had committed suicide was in conflict with the testimony John Lawton had given:

Gentlemen you have heard it asserted this day that this truly ill-fated girl had committed suicide; but if that be so, it appears exceedingly strange that, immediately on the prisoner abruptly quitting the barn and leaving her alone, she should have used such various instruments in order to destroy herself; for it appears that she must have fired a pistol and, either before or after she discharged it, must have stabbed herself, in various parts of the body, with some sharp instrument.

At 1425, after thirty-five minutes of deliberation, the jury returned to the court. It was their unanimous opinion that William Corder had murdered Maria Marten. The judge had no option but to pass the death sentence:

My advice to you is, not to flatter yourself with the slightest hope of mercy on earth. You sent this unfortunate young woman to her account, with all her imperfections upon her head, without allowing her any time for preparation. She had not time to lift up her eyes to a throne of grace, to implore mercy and forgiveness for her manifold transgressions – she had no time allowed her to repent of her sins – no time granted to throw herself upon her knees, to implore pardon at the Eternal Throne! The same measure which you meted to her is not meted out to you again. A small interval is allowed you for preparation. Let me earnestly entreat you to use it well – the scene of this world closes upon you – but, I hope, another and a better world will open to your view. Remember the lessons of religion, which you, doubtless, received in your childhood – consider the effects which may be produced by a hearty and sincere repentance – listen to the voice of the ministers of religion who will, I trust, advise and console you, so that you may be able to meet with becoming resignation and fortitude that dreadful ordeal which you will have shortly to undergo. Nothing remains now for me to do but to pass upon you the awful sentence of the law, and that sentence is – That you be taken back to the prison from whence you came, and that you be taken from thence, on Monday next, to a place of Execution, and that you there be hanged by the Neck until you are Dead; and that your body shall afterwards be dissected and anatomized; and may the Lord God Almighty, of his infinite goodness, have mercy on your soul.

Corder broke down and he was placed under constant watch

back in jail. Over the next few days he spent time with the prison governor, John Orridge and the prison chaplain, the Revd W. Stocking. He was due to be executed just after noon on 11 August 1828, three days after the end of the trial.
He wrote a last letter to his wife:

> *My life's loved Companion, – I am now going to the scaffold and I have a lively hope of obtaining mercy and pardon for my numerous offences. May Heaven bless and protect you throughout this transitory vale of misery, and when we meet again, may it be in the regions of bliss! Adieu, my love, adieu! In less than an hour I hope to be in Heaven. My last prayer is that God will endue you with patience, fortitude, and resignation to his Divine will – rest assured that his wise providence will work all things together for your good. The awful sentence which has been passed upon me, and which I am now summoned to answer, I confess is very just, and I die on peace with all mankind. I feel truly grateful for the kindnesses I have received from Mr. Orridge, and for the religious instruction and consolation I have received from the Reverend Mr. Stocking, who has promised to take my last words to you. Adieu – W. C.*

The confession made by Corder was timed at 2330 on Sunday evening, 10 August in Bury jail. It was taken in the condemned cell, witnessed by Orridge, Stocking and the under sheriff, Timothy Holmes. In it Corder admitted to the shooting of Maria with a pistol, that he had borrowed a spade, dug a hole and had collected a pickaxe from his home to dig a bigger hole. He had dragged the body by a handkerchief tied round the neck. He visited the barn the next day to wash blood from the barn floor.

The signed confession only covered part of the story. Corder denied that he had stabbed Maria and he went to his maker without telling anyone the full truth.

It is not just his descendents that believe that Corder did not receive a fair trial and that his sentence and execution were driven primarily by press interest. For one thing the press painted him as something of a monster. This seems to be more than unfair as he stood by Maria Marten when she fell pregnant with his child. Throughout the case, particularly before the trial, the press coverage was never kind to Corder. Many believe that this factor alone prejudiced a fair outcome and drove the jury to

Moyse's Hall, Bury St Edmunds, on market day.

convict and for the execution to take place in undignified haste.

Much of the evidence against Corder was circumstantial. There were mistakes made during the trial and the prosecution was adept at manipulating statements made by witnesses to implicate Corder. Perhaps the most perplexing part of the whole case is the role of Ann Marten, Maria's stepmother. It is perfectly possible that she was having an affair with Corder, after all she was not much older than Maria herself. It seems coincidental and rather convenient that Ann Marten's dreams began just a few days after Corder had married Mary Moore. It does beg the question whether the news of the marriage had reached Polstead. If it had then there was a very good reason for Ann Marten to behave as she did, as she must have suspected that her relationship with Corder would be over.

The infamous Red Barn murder was one of a handful of cases that created immense public interest. While Corder was waiting for his trial, plays were being performed and songs composed, speculating about his involvement in the killing. At the annual fair at Polstead on the 16 to 17 July, just a fortnight or more before the trial, there were two theatrical representations of 'the late murder of Maria Marten'. In one of the exhibits there was a scene entitled 'The Red Barn'. In the exhibit there were effigies, one of which was a mutilated body lying on the floor, surrounded by the coroner and the jury during the inquest. It purported to show exactly how they had appeared on that Sunday, 20 April, the day after Maria Marten's body was found. The exhibits enraged William Corder's mother and she lodged a complaint on the basis that her son would never get a fair trial under these circumstances.

By mid-August 1828 even the Red Barn itself had been plundered. The boards had been removed to the height of 6 feet, however the only known surviving modern day relic is in the Moyse's Hall collection, a wooden shoe-shaped snuffbox. There is also an iron stay from the barn doors, which is held in a private collection.

Maria Marten's body was buried in Polstead churchyard shortly after the inquest in 1827, although it was exhumed and used as an exhibit at the trial. The body was re-interred, but after a short while the headstone completely disappeared after thousands of souvenir hunters had taken away fragments of it. The case spawned Staffordshire pottery, penny dreadfuls, more plays and printed broadsheets.

Sign to Polstead, near Bury St Edmunds.

Linda Nessworthy, amongst many others, maintains that Corder was innocent. An interesting point is that the prosecutor in Corder's trial was the same man that had presided over the inquest. Whilst accepting that Corder admitted there was a scuffle and the gun went off, Nessworthy believes that it was not a premeditated murder.

Certainly at the time Maria Marten was painted as some kind of virtuous simple village girl. The popular view created by the press was that Corder had seduced her and when he tired of her the black-hearted villain killed her. The pictures painted either by the press or by the plays and songs of the time illustrated the pair as archetypal melodrama characters. Maria Marten, the cruelly treated maiden and William Corder, the unscrupulous black-hearted squire.

In James Curtis's book *The Mysterious Murder of Maria Marten* a credible suspect had emerged. His name was Samuel Beauty Smith. He was a notorious thief, a pimp and a card shark. He had been a dealer in stolen goods around Polstead. Corder had fallen in with him through a prostitute with the improbable name of Hannah Fandango.

Corder and Smith had spent time together in London pubs and brothels before his relationship with Maria. Corder had scraped together cash through fraud and when it ran out so did his friends. Corder found himself back at the family farm; then there was the pregnant local girl.

Curtis reported that on one occasion Corder had told a farmhand 'I'll give you a pound note to cut my throat'. At the time the farmhand thought he was joking and laughed it off. What if Smith had either taken it upon himself to free his friend, or had done the deed in return for payment from Corder?

CHAPTER 2

The Bootlace Murders

The murder of Mary Bennett
– Great Yarmouth, 1900

Herbert John Bennett was born in Gravesend, Kent in 1880. His contemporaries described him as being rather intelligent, despite the fact that he had had very little formal schooling. His father was a foreman at a cement works, but Bennett spurned this occupation, first becoming a newspaper seller and later an assistant in a grocer's shop. In 1896, he had met the 19 year old Mary Jane Clark and his life was now heading for a fateful end some five years later at the end of a rope in Norwich.

Throughout his life, it seems that Bennett was not averse to perverting the truth for his own purposes. Indeed, this less than saintly figure had a colourful history, all seemingly designed to provide him with riches beyond his imaginings. It is also clear that Mary Jane Clark was a willing accomplice in many of Bennett's illegal schemes.

When Bennett met Clark she was living with her grandmother in Northfleet. He would walk from his home in Swanscombe in order to meet her when she left chapel on a Sunday. Bennett had met Clark after replying to her advertisement offering music lessons for the violin and piano. She was slightly over 5 feet tall with titian, shoulder-length hair; she wore glasses and was slightly deaf. Bennett was her first pupil.

Despite the fact that Clark's parents were in opposition to her marrying a shop assistant with the Northfleet Co-Operative Stores, earning just 15s per week, the inevitable happened and their daughter fell pregnant. Despite the impending birth, Bennett's parents were set against their son marrying the girl and the proposed ceremony in Northfleet church was scuppered by Bennett's own father telling the vicar that his son had made a false declaration about his age. Bennett and Clark were not to be swayed from their decision and they were married on 22 July 1897 at Leyton Registry Office near Mary's grandparents' home.

Soon after the wedding Bennett lost his job with the Co-Op and seemed to be content with wandering around the local marshland with his shotgun. It is unclear whether Clark's child was stillborn or died a few days after it was born. Whatever the circumstances, this does seem to have released some of the tension between the young couple and Clark's parents with whom they had been living since the wedding. They then moved to West Ham to live with Clark's grandmother. The old lady died in April 1898 leaving Clark her much-treasured gold necklace, which was to play an important role much later in this story. She wore this alongside a silver watch, which had been given to her by her father for her twelfth birthday. No sooner had the old lady died than Bennett and Clark's father started to argue about the dead woman's possessions. It was said that Bennett actually threatened his father-in-law with a shotgun. This appears to have severed the links between Mary and the rest of her family, mirroring the lack of communication between Bennett and his father.

The young married couple seem to have then embarked on a career based on fraud. They would purchase cheap violins through the *Exchange and Mart* for around 4s 6d which they would then re-advertise with Mary posing as a distraught and poverty-stricken clergyman's daughter or, in other instances, a widow. She would claim sometimes that her husband was a gifted, professional musician who had suddenly died, leaving her with the only option of selling his most treasured possession, the violin. After all, she had small children to feed and no other means of income. In this way she would sell the violins for one or two guineas each. In October 1898 Mary had the additional prop in order to fool the unsuspecting buyers as her daughter Ruby had just been born.

It seems very clear that the couple made a considerable amount of money from the sale of these violins because in early 1900 Bennett was able to buy a grocers' shop in Westgate-on-Sea. He paid £375 of the £450 asking price for the business in cash. It is here that accounts begin to diverge. Either Bennett kept the shop for just eight days, or, in other accounts, two months. What is certain is that the grocery business was completely destroyed by a mysterious fire. Bennett had taken the sensible precaution, of course, of insuring it with the Kent Insurance Company. He managed to make a tidy sum despite the fact that his insurance claim was originally turned down. It is probable that he received over £200 for the building in addition to the £450 he received for the loss of his horse, cart, stock and piano. It should be pointed out that most of this stock had been purchased on credit and Bennett hadn't paid for it yet.

The couple seem to have used the proceeds to purchase tickets on a steamer bound for Cape Town. They left Ruby with Bennett's grandfather in Gravesend with the story that they were going to North America. Bennett purchased the tickets in the name of Mr and Mrs Hood on 7 March; he paid for a single fare costing around £45 for the two-berth cabin on SS *Gaika*. Strangely, he also purchased in London a false moustache and wig for himself and a blonde wig for Mary. Exactly why the couple went to Cape Town is unknown, but his defence counsel in the trial, Sir Edward Marshall Hall, told the court that Bennett had gone to South Africa as he had been engaged as a spy for the Boers. Whatever actually happened in South Africa does not seem to have come to a great deal as they only stayed in Cape Town for four days before heading back on another ship, returning to London on 9 May. Initially they moved into 64 Wickham Lane, Plumstead, which was a boarding house owned by Emma Elliston who was the wife of a police constable. Mary originally booked the rooms and Bennett arrived later in the evening. Mary then left to collect Ruby and the three of them were installed by 12 May. Mrs Elliston later testified that she believed the couple to be on particularly bad terms with one another. She described Bennett as being rather aggressive towards his wife and on at least one occasion Mary had told her that her husband had struck her. Indeed when Mary had arrived with the child, Bennett was angry that she had taken so long. Mary was heard to say 'You knew the time I should come. Why did you not come and meet me? What with carrying the baby and the luggage, I could not get here any sooner.' Elliston testified that Bennett replied 'Damn you, and the baby too'. Throughout their stay Elliston claimed that Mary always appeared to be affectionate and kindly towards her husband but she did hear Mary say to Bennett 'Herbert, I shall always follow you for the sake of the child and if you are not careful I will get you fifteen years'. Bennett was heard to reply 'I wish you were dead. And if you are not careful you soon will be.' Elliston also heard Bennett tell Mary to find a house in Bexley Heath 'I have a berth at Woolwich. From tonight I do not wish to live with you again.'

Whatever the truth or fiction behind the quarrels between Bennett and Mary, what is clear is that by the middle of June both had left Mrs Elliston's house. It seems that the couple and their child stayed with a Mrs MacDonald at 10 Woolwich Road but, by this time, specifically 12 June, Bennett, posing as a bachelor, also lived at 41 Union Street, Woolwich. By July, however, Mary and the child moved into 1 Glencoe Villas, Izane Road, Bexley Heath. She paid three months' rent in advance and clinched possession of a semi-detached house by producing a reference signed by W. A. Phillips. It had actually been written by Bennett himself who, after spending three weeks working for the Co-Operative Society in Woolwich, leaving their employment on 29 June, had been temporarily unemployed until 16 July when he was working as a labourer at the Woolwich Arsenal for some 30s a week. At this time he was living in Union Street, Woolwich with a landlady called Mrs Pankhurst.

By all accounts Bennett did not make many visits to Glencoe Villas to see his wife and child. Money was an immediate problem; not only was he paying for the rent on the house in Izane Road but he was also having to find money for Mrs Pankhurst and he was, by then, also seeing another woman. He had met Alice Meadows on 1 July when he had accompanied a friend and fellow lodger called Stevens to London. Alice was a friend of Stevens's fiancée. She was a parlour maid employed by a family near Hyde Park and was immediately smitten by Bennett. He told her that he had been a grocer's assistant and was single, independently wealthy through inheritance and now was a profitable second-hand violin tradesman. He told Alice that his cousin Fred lived with his wife and child in Bexley Heath and on occasion he would have to go and visit them. They exchanged a number of affectionate letters and saw one another regularly on a Thursday and a Sunday.

Bennett wanted to take Alice away during her fortnight's holiday and was keen to take her to Ireland. In the event she finally agreed to go to Great Yarmouth with Bennett for a weekend. One of Alice's work colleagues knew the addresses of some respectable accommodation in Great Yarmouth and Bennett wrote to Mrs Rudrum in order to enquire whether she had any vacancies. As it was a bank holiday weekend she replied in the negative, so on Saturday, 4 August they travelled first class by train to Great Yarmouth and stayed in separate rooms at the Crown and Anchor Hotel. What is particularly significant about this weekend is that it not only allayed the fears of Alice about going away to Ireland for a fortnight with Bennett, but what also stood out was the fact that Bennett was particularly

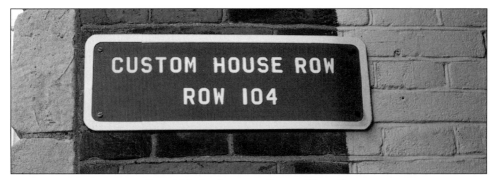

Row 104, also known as Custom House Row.

The ornate entrance to Row 104, next to the former Port Authority building.

scathing about the Rows area of the town. At the time there were 129 narrow lanes where the houses were so close together that you could reach across the alleyways and touch the buildings on either side. Bennett told Alice that he was extremely pleased that they had not chosen to stay in number 3, Row 104, which was Mrs Rudrum's house.

They arrived back in London on the Sunday. On Thursday 9 August Alice sent Bennett a telegram wishing him many happy returns as it was his birthday, but also on that day he received another telegram, which was delivered to his lodgings. It was opened by Mrs Pankhurst and it read 'Try to come home M very ill'. Mary's next-door neighbour had sent it. Mrs Pankhurst took the telegram directly to Bennett at the Woolwich Arsenal and he explained to her that M was his cousin who lived in Bexley. That night he visited Glencoe Villas by bicycle and he returned to Woolwich the following morning with a woman's umbrella and no bicycle. Bennett told Mrs Pankhurst that his cousin was terminally ill with influenza and that it was not expected that she would live much longer.

Bennett continued his affair with Alice Meadows and on 28 August they left for their fortnight's holiday in Killarney in Ireland. It seems that Bennett was flush with cash as they travelled by first class, stayed in respectable hotels and wined and dined every night. When they returned to England on 11 September Alice was the proud possessor of a diamond and ruby ring given to her by Bennett as a token of his love and intention to marry her the following June. At all times during the holiday it appears that Bennett was the perfect gentleman and never forced his attentions on Alice, content only to be in her company. Bennett even introduced Alice as his fiancée to Mrs Pankhurst. Bennett returned to work, as did a happy Alice.

On Friday, 14 September Bennett visited Glencoe Villas and it seems that plans had been made with his wife, as she hurriedly went shopping with her neighbour, Lillian Langman, for clothes, which included a blouse and a veil. Bennett was a busy man on the 14th as he also managed to tell Alice Meadows that he would not be able to see her the next day because he had to travel to Gravesend to see his ailing grandfather.

On Saturday, 15 September Bennett again visited Glencoe Villas, having told the Woolwich Arsenal that he was ill. Soon after he left his wife, Mary also left the house, telling her neighbour, Lillian Langman, that she was going on holiday with her husband. She said 'My old man is going to take me after all, we're going to Yorkshire'. Mrs Langman was sure from what she had said that she was going to Leeds. After asking her neighbour to look after her dog, Mary locked up the house and took Ruby, a brown bag and a brown paper parcel away with her. Mrs Langman also noted that Mary was wearing her treasured gold chain.

At 9 p.m. that Saturday night Mary arrived at Mrs Rudrum's house in Great Yarmouth, purporting to be a Mrs Hood. Mrs Rudrum distinctly remembered seeing a man walk into the Row with Mary but when she opened the door only Mary and Ruby were there. Mary settled into the room and put the child to bed, immediately leaving on her own and not returning until nearly midnight. Mrs Rudrum saw that she was rather drunk and it was at this stage that Mary told her that she came from York, was a widow and that her husband had died three months before her child had been born. She told Mrs Rudrum that she had been drinking with her brother-in-law and that he was a jealous man who tended to follow her around. The same night Bennett had checked into the Crown and Anchor Hotel in Great Yarmouth but had left early the following morning, catching the 7.30 a.m. train, which arrived in London at 11.30 a.m. At noon he had visited Alice Meadow's mother's house at 22 York Road, Stepney and spoke to Mrs Lenston who also lived there.

On the Monday Bennett was back at work at Woolwich Arsenal and at some point during that week he encountered two friends that had worked with him at the Co-Operative Stores. They asked after his wife and child and he tearfully explained to them that they had both died in South Africa from the fever. Bennett told them 'Don't say much about it, as I feel it very much. She was my right hand'. On the Wednesday Bennett made the journey to Glencoe Villas and asked if anyone had been to visit the house. On the Thursday he told a disappointed Alice that he would not be able to see her on the following Sunday because his grandfather in Gravesend had worsened and that he was honour-bound to see the old man. It is probable that Bennett was in London until at least the afternoon of Saturday, 22 September because Mrs Pankhurst saw him in Union Street carrying a railway timetable and wearing a light grey suit. Also on Saturday Bennett rearranged plans by telephone with Alice, confirming that he would not be able to meet her and her brother on the river on Sunday but would, instead, see her outside her place of work at 3.30 p.m.

Meanwhile, in Great Yarmouth, Mary had been returning to Mrs Rudrum's house at around 9 p.m. each evening. When she went out on Friday 21st she told Mrs Rudrum that she was expecting to receive a letter that day. Mary did not return until 10.45 that night and Mrs Rudrum's daughter, Alice, was sure that she had seen a man standing with her at the bottom of the Row. She even claimed to have heard the man say to Mary 'You understand, don't you, I am placed in an awkward position just now.' This was followed by a kissing sound. There was indeed a letter waiting for Mrs Hood, or Mary. It was postmarked Woolwich and simply said 'Meet me under the big clock and put your baby to bed.' It was signed 'Hood'. Mary explained to Mrs Rudrum that the letter had come from her brother-in-law who had been trying to find her a house in London.

On the following day Mary went out for the morning but was in Mrs Rudrum's home throughout the afternoon, only leaving again at 6.30 p.m. Mrs Rudrum testified that Mary was wearing her gold brooch, her long gold chain, five rings and, as it would later turn out, her treasured silver watch and a considerable sum of money in her purse. Alice Rudrum encountered Mary outside the Town Hall at around 9 p.m. and a witness called Mr Borking who managed the South Quay Distillery in Great Yarmouth saw her again. He was later able to identify both Mary and the man who he said accompanied her, as Bennett. This was at about 10

Great Yarmouth Town Hall.

p.m. and Mr Borking was somewhat surprised to see two strangers in the pub that was normally a local only used by fishermen and their wives. He described the man as having a large moustache, which he kept stroking. The man drank whisky and the woman gin. At some point Mary's male companion looked at a railway timetable and they stayed in the pub for some time, leaving together. Mr Borking was the last person to see Mary alive, apart, of course, from her murderer.

At about 11 p.m. a man by the name of Alfred Marks or Mason was enjoying a courtship with his girlfriend, Blanche Smith, on the south beach at Great Yarmouth. The night was dark, dry and warm and they distinctly heard scuffling noises nearby and assumed it was another courting couple. They also heard a woman's voice moaning 'Mercy, mercy'. About ten minutes later they left the beach and happened to pass a man and woman. The man looked up and glared at them and they could also see that the woman was lying on her back on the sand.

A waiter by the name of Reade testified that at 11.30 p.m., a dishevelled and out of breath man arrived at the Crown and Anchor Hotel. Reade recognized him as the same Mr Bennett that had stayed there before. The man explained that he had just missed the last tram from Gorleston and that he would have to leave early on the Sunday morning to catch the 7.20 train to London. Whether this was Bennett or not, a man in a light-grey suit and a soft trilby hat was seen by a local newsagent, Mr Headley, standing beside the open door of a third class compartment at the station. Mr Headley also described the man as being rather nervous and agitated. If this was Bennett, he probably had good reason to be both.

At around 6 a.m. on Sunday, 23rd John Lawton left his home at 36 Boreham Road and walked along Barrack Road towards the seafront. He was a bathing hut boy and when he reached the South Denes area of the beach he angled off towards the bathing huts. It was then that he noticed what appeared to be a woman asleep on the sand. He met his employer, Mr Briers, and mentioned that he had seen a sleeping woman. Mr Briers suggested that as this was not really the done thing, and in any case the local council frowned upon using the beach as a bedroom, that Lawton should go and wake her up.

As Lawton approached the sleeping woman he could see that she was lying on her back and just as he was about to shake her shoulder, it became clear that the woman was dead. She had been strangled with a mohair bootlace. It had been drawn so

The sand dunes of South Denes in Great Yarmouth,
where both murders took place.

tight around her neck that it was embedded in the flesh. What was peculiar was the knot, which was a reef knot with a granny knot above it. The woman's face was bruised and scratched, her fingers were clenched, her skirt and petticoat had been dragged up over her knees and there were bloodstains on her under-clothes. Lawton had seen enough and ran into the town, happening upon PC Manship. The constable described the woman as wearing a light grey skirt and jacket, which was trimmed with white braid and she was also wearing a white blouse and a green tie. Beside the body was a sailor's hat with a black band as well as a black veil with white spots. He found a pair of kid gloves in the pocket of her jacket. PC Manship described the woman's hair as being titian in colour and she was wearing five rings, three on her left hand and two on her right. There was no other jewellery on the body.

Mrs Rudrum had already reported the fact that one of her guests was missing. Very quickly the local police were able to link the two incidents and Inspector Lingwood made haste to investigate the disappearance of Mrs Hood. Lingwood searched Mrs Hood's bedroom, finding little of immediate significance, except half a first class railway ticket from Liverpool Street Station, a gold brooch with the word 'baby' engraved on it, a small purse containing a latch key and two pieces of baby's clothing with a laundry mark which read '599'. Significantly Lingwood also discovered a photograph of the mysterious Mrs Hood and her baby that had been taken by a beach photographer the Thursday before. The photograph clearly showed her gold chain which had not been found on the body, neither had the watch, which Mrs Rudrum had seen the last time Mary left the house.

The police circulated the photograph of Mrs Hood and set police forces all around the country to discover the identity of the laundry mark. However, by the end of October no progress had been made and at the coroner's inquest the jury agreed on a verdict of 'wilful murder by person or persons unknown'.

Mary Jane Clark was buried as Mrs Hood at St Nicholas Church, Great Yarmouth, witnessed by a huge crowd of sightseers.

Bennett, wearing his grey suit and a bowler hat, encountered Alice Meadows in Hyde Park at 1 p.m. on Sunday, 23 September. She was amazed to see him as she believed that he was still in Gravesend. He explained that all of his relatives were in Gravesend and that he had come specifically to see her as he would have to return to Woolwich as soon as possible. He declined the offer of having either lunch or dinner at Alice's mother's house. As far as this is concerned, Bennett was not lying. He did go to Woolwich where Mrs Pankhurst, who commented on the fact that he was wearing the same suit that he had worn the previous day, saw him. That night or, more probably, the following day he wrote a letter to Alice, it read:

My own darling Alice,

I received your kind and loving letter this evening, and was quite pleased to hear from you, as it cheers me up. I arrived home quite safe but was not at all happy. I am glad you had somebody to pass the time away with, dearest, as you would have felt very miserable after seeing me as you did. I shall be very glad indeed, my darling, when you do not have to leave me at all, for I feel quite miserable now that I have had to wait so long to see you.

I shall be up on Thursday evening, dearest, all being well, as I am now on day work, and I hope I shall keep at day work as it is much better.

I have been to Bexley tonight, dear, and am sorry to tell you that grandfather passed away this morning, at 3.30 am and is to be buried on Monday next, when I shall not be able to attend as I must not lose any more time at present.

I hope you are feeling better, darling, and I shall be glad to see you out of the place altogether. Give my love to mother and all at home when you write. Hoping they are all quite well, I must now close, my dearest, as it is getting late. Hoping to see you on Thursday when I shall have lots of news.

With kindest love and kisses, I remain your most loving and affectionate

Herbert

Bennett followed up the 'disposal' of his grandfather as far as Alice was concerned with a similar treatment to his cousin in Bexley. He told Mrs Pankhurst that he had given his cousin, Fred, £15 to take his family to South Africa.

On Wednesday, 26 September Bennett visited Glencoe Villas, terminated the tenancy in writing to the landlord, explaining that he was emigrating to America and, at the same time, told Mrs Langman that his wife was ill in Yorkshire. While he was at Glencoe Villas he collected some of Mary's clothes, which he later gave to Alice on the pretext that this was his cousin Fred's wife's clothes and that she would not need these warm clothes in such a warmer climate. When he saw Alice on that Wednesday he also told her that he wished to move the date of their wedding forward to Christmas. He also gave her a gold brooch in the shape of a pickaxe and shovel, which had belonged to his wife Mary and he explained that he had arranged to buy his cousin Fred's furniture so that they could settle down as soon as they were married.

As for the Glencoe Villas' lease, the agents told Bennett that he would have to give three months' notice. It was finally agreed that he should pay £4 10s in settlement and he told the landlord and house agents that his wife had left the house for health reasons.

On Sunday, 30th he again met Alice Meadows who joyfully agreed to marry him at Christmas. Bennett gave her a blue coat and skirt in which she could be wed, a sealskin cape, some lace, a tablecloth, a silver brooch and some dress material. All of these items had belonged to his wife.

Sometime in early October Bennett bumped into a man called Mr Parritt who vaguely knew him and asked after his wife and child. Bennett gave the stock answer that they had died of a fever in South Africa and that he was really too distraught about the matter to talk more of it. On 6 October he returned again to Glencoe Villas to collect his wife's dog and he told Mrs Langman that his wife was still seriously ill and had asked him to collect her dog and take it with him to Leeds. On 17 October Alice Meadows gave up her job as a parlour maid and was taken to Charlton by Bennett to see a house, which her fiancé thought would be a suitable matrimonial home. Bennett paid a deposit on the house to secure it for his future wife.

It is not entirely clear how by early November the police had finally made a link between Mrs Hood and Woolwich. It appears that Mrs Rudrum and her daughter Alice had remembered that the letter Mrs Hood had received the day before she had been killed had a Woolwich postmark. By all accounts no one was using 599 as their laundry mark but enquiries in the Bexley Heath area revealed the fact that on 5 November a Mrs Bennett was reported missing. The link was quickly made between the laundry mark and Glencoe Villas. Neighbours were shown the beach photograph and it quickly emerged that Mrs Hood and Mrs Bennett were, indeed, the same woman. Chief Inspector Leach of Scotland Yard was told that Bennett worked for the Co-Operative Stores and eventually spoke to a friend and co-employee of Bennett's called Robert Allen. He, too, was able to identify the photograph as that of being Mrs Bennett and her child. Allen recounted to the Chief Inspector that sometime in the previous month he had met Bennett by chance and agreed to buy a bicycle from him. He had agreed to meet Bennett at Glencoe Villas, which Bennett had explained was his cousin's house. Bennett also showed him a piano, which he also offered for sale. Allen claimed to have asked 'Is your wife here?' to which Bennett had replied 'She is not here. She is down home.' Later, he told the Chief Inspector, Bennett had told him 'I have no wife, but I am about to be married'. Allen was confused; he had met a woman with Bennett who he was sure had been introduced to him as Bennett's wife. In the event, Allen had agreed to pay £23 for both the bicycle and the piano. Curiously Bennett had produced a receipt for fifteen guineas, telling Allen that this was what he had paid for the bicycle. Allen checked the price with the manufacturers, who told him that this was a grossly inflated price and not the recommended retail price. He accused Bennett of forging a receipt for the bicycle and refused to pay him more than £6 for it.

Leach was very interested in meeting Mr Bennett and Allen was able to furnish him with his current address. On 8 November Leach waited for Bennett to leave his job at the Woolwich Arsenal. Allen introduced Leach as a Mr Brown. As he put his arm around Bennett's shoulder, he told Bennett 'I am a police officer and I arrest you for the murder of Mrs Hood on Yarmouth beach'. Bennett was stunned and replied 'I do not understand what you mean'. Bennett was taken by Leach and a police sergeant to Woolwich Police Station where he was formally arrested, to which he replied 'I have not been to

Yarmouth. I have not lived with my wife since January, when I found a lot of letters from another man in her pocket.' When shown the beach photograph Bennett told the two police officers that he did not recognize the woman or the child.

The police's next move was to search Bennett's room at 18 William Street under the watchful eyes of Mrs Pankhurst. They found a portmanteau with a label from the *Avondale Castle*, presumably the return ship that Bennett and his wife had used when returning from South Africa. In it they found a false moustache, a man's and a woman's wig, a revolver and cartridges, a receipt for Glencoe Villas, collars marked 599, two pearl necklaces and fourteen letters from Alice Meadows. The most damning evidence not only linked Bennett with Great Yarmouth but also with the mysterious Mrs Hood. In triumph Leach pulled out a receipt from the Crown and Anchor Hotel in Great Yarmouth for the period that Bennett had stayed there with Alice, along with a long, gold necklace and a silver watch.

In due course, the Rudrums were shown the watch and chain and they were able to identify them as those worn by Mrs Hood. They were also asked whether the name Bennett meant anything to them and not only could they produce Bennett's letter asking for lodgings back in the early summer, but could now positively assert that it was the same handwriting that they had seen on the letter sent to Mrs Hood on the day before her death.

By 17 November the newspapers were full of stories regarding the case and certainly the feelings against him in Great Yarmouth were very ugly. When Bennett was brought before the Great Yarmouth Magistrates at the Town Hall, a mob tried to lynch him. However, Bennett remained relaxed and throughout the whole of the four-day hearing he was happy to smile for the newspaper cameramen. The *Evening News* reported 'His thin lips nervously twitched as the charge against him was read.' The *Daily Mail* said of him:

> He has a good forehead, with wavy, dark brown hair, a long nose which is straight except for a slight tilt at the end, brown eyes which are a trifle near together, large unshapely ears and a slightly receding chin. He had neglected to get his hands clean before coming to court.

Characteristically Bennett had pleaded not guilty; he only showed a moment of concern when the magistrates committed him to trial for the murder.

The *Evening News*, it is said, much prejudiced the case against Bennett before he came to trial on 26 February 1901 at The Central Criminal Court at the Old Bailey. The newspaper had interviewed Allen, Mrs Elliston and one of Bennett's former landladies, Mrs Cato. Mrs Cato could throw light on Bennett's fraudulent sale of violins and even said, when talking about a murder, that Bennett had suggested:

> *There is only one way to do a job of that kind. Strangle them.*
> *It is quick and silent.*

As far as the *Evening News* was concerned Bennett was guilty. They even managed to organize an interview with Alice Meadows; the reporter in the most flowery prose described Alice as:

> *Prostrated with grief and hesitating between love and duty, doubtful as to whether to screen the man she loves from the merciless clutches of the law, or whether to aid justice in its demand that the woman done to death on the sands at Yarmouth be avenged.*

Originally the trial was to be held in Norwich at the Norfolk County Assizes. Bennett's solicitor, the Tunbridge Wells based E. Elvy Robb, claimed that he could not agree to a trial in Norfolk as his client would be disadvantaged due to the local feelings against him. It also made sense that since a large number of the witnesses were London-based that the case should be transferred to the Old Bailey, to be heard before the Lord Chief Justice Lord Alverstone.

Bennett's defence counsel was the famed advocate Marshall Hall and Charles Gill led the prosecution. Marshall Hall clearly believed in his client's innocence and in one conversation with Thorn Drury, a junior counsel, the young man said 'My God, I believe that man's innocent'. Marshall Hall replied 'Of course he is innocent'.

From the outset of the trial Marshall Hall made strenuous efforts to undermine the testimony of each of the prosecution witnesses. It was clear that the most damning evidence was the watch and chain. He was also concerned about the evidence related to Bennett's visits to Great Yarmouth and the callous way that he had disposed of his wife's assets after her death. Above all, Bennett had a motive; his affair and proposed marriage to

Alice Meadows. On the other hand, as far as Alice was concerned, Bennett was a perfect gentleman. Marshall Hall faced a huge list of prosecution witnesses but was able to use the fact that so much information had been given in the newspapers to his advantage. When he cross-examined Mrs Elliston about the evidence she had given regarding Bennett's behaviour towards his wife, Marshall Hall held little back:

Marshall Hall – Do you read the *Evening News* and the *Daily Mail*?
Elliston – I have been worried too much to do so lately.
M.H. – Did you see a statement of yours about November last?
Elliston – I saw it in the papers.
M.H. – Did you read the statement as an account of what you knew about this case in the *Daily Mail* of November 12th?
Elliston – I saw it in some evening paper.
M.H. – Were you one of the first people to recognize the photograph of the deceased as being Mrs Bennett?
Elliston – Yes.
M.H. – Were you much visited by people representing newspapers?
Elliston – There were only one or two.
M.H. – Did you speak freely to them?
Elliston – I did not say much to them.
M.H. – Did you tell them this, that when Mrs Bennett arrived at your house she was richly dressed and wearing a quantity of jewellery?
Elliston – I did not say she was wearing a quantity of jewellery; I said she was dressed well, but not richly dressed. I said her bodice was lined with silk but not her dresses. I said she had a lot of jewellery. She had gold spectacles, ornaments in her hair, a gold bracelet and rings.
M.H. – Did you say her underwear was covered with lace?
Elliston – I saw her underclothes were good and had lace on them.
M.H. – Did you say to the reporter that her purse was observed to be well filled with gold.
Elliston – Yes. She had plenty of money.
The Judge – What were they paying you a week?
Elliston – Ten shillings a week for the apartments.
M.H. – Did you tell the press that you did not believe the story that they had come from South Africa?
Elliston – I did not say I did not believe it.

M.H. – Did you say they did not look like people who had come off a sea voyage?

Elliston – I do not remember.

M.H. – That must have been an invention of the gentlemen of the press?

Elliston – I suppose so.

M.H. – Did you see an account, purporting to be an account of what you had said to a reporter, in an evening paper?

Elliston – I read something in an evening paper, but I do not know when it was.

M.H. – Did your husband actually go the police station to see Bennett the night he was arrested?

Elliston – Yes, he went there to identify him.

M.H. – Knowing that on 6th November this man had been arrested on the charge of murder, on 11th November you were gossiping about this case to a newspaper man?

Elliston – I did not think it would do Bennett any harm.

M.H. (holding up a copy of the *Evening News*): And you as a woman will say that you did not tell the man what appeared in the paper?

Admittedly, Mrs Elliston's husband was a police constable so he would have been able to give an unimpeachable identification of Bennett. Nevertheless, damage had been done to this witness's testimony. There was amusement too during the trial, particularly when the prosecution, denying that William Simmons, Bennett's grandfather, was dead, called him to testify. He was asked by Gill 'And is it not true that you were to be buried on September 24th?'

Mrs Pankhurst could not be shaken from her testimony that Bennett had not slept at his lodgings on 22 September. She even told the court that her son had gone upstairs with a cup of tea for Bennett on Sunday morning, but had returned with it not drunk, as Bennett was not there. Bennett's two friends from the Co-Operative Stores, Mr Cameron and Mr Parritt similarly resisted all of Marshall Hall's attempts to induce them to change their story that Bennett was with them on the evening of 29 September, as Bennett had claimed that it was in fact the night of the 22nd when he was with them.

Marshall Hall tried a different tack with Robert Allen, beginning with the statement that Allen owed Bennett money from the bicycle and piano transaction:

M.H. – You owe him £17.

Allen – There is that to pay over the piano and bicycle transaction.

M.H. – Have you said that if Bennett worried you for the money you would prosecute him for fraud?

Allen – No.

M.H. – Did you say the cycle receipt was forged?

Allen – Yes.

M.H. – Do you want to have your revenge on this man who had swindled you over the bicycle by having him arrested in the street?

Allen – I had no idea of having revenge.

M.H. – You got the piano and the bicycle and you propose to keep them?

Allen – I have them still, and I do not know what I shall do with them. I had an expert to examine the piano and he said it was not worth the price.

M.H. – And yet you agreed to buy it?

Mr Borking, the pub landlord in Great Yarmouth, the waiter at the Crown and Anchor and the newsagent on Great Yarmouth railway station all testified that they recognized Bennett as having been in the town both on 22 and 23 September. A Mrs Gibson, the wife of a fisherman who was in the South Quay Distillery on the Saturday night, was slightly unsure that the man sitting with Mary was actually Bennett. This was largely on account of the fact that the man that she had seen had a heavier moustache. Marshall Hall accused Mr Reade, the waiter at the Crown and Anchor Hotel, of only having come forward to identify Bennett after having seen articles in the press. As far as the newsagent was concerned, Marshall Hall managed to convince the man to admit that the person that he had seen standing in the doorway of the third class compartment only looked like Bennett. All of these witnesses had told the court that Bennett was wearing a trilby hat. In fact Bennett only ever wore a bowler hat and indeed he was wearing the self-same hat when he met Alice Meadows that Sunday afternoon.

Mrs Rudrum's testimony could have proved to have been decisive in either acquitting or condemning Marshall Hall's client. She told the court that the letter that Mrs Hood had received on the Friday before her death had been postmarked from Woolwich, and that she had produced a letter from

Bennett enquiring about a room earlier in the summer. She had also found a petticoat in a drawer in her house which had been missed by the police. It was marked with ink and bore the word 'Benet'. Marshall Hall then began to direct his line of enquiry to prove the fact that Mrs Rudrum herself had created the petticoat evidence. First he asked her to spell the name Bennett and she replied 'Bennet' and then said that the name should have another 't' on the end of it. The defence counsel could smell blood and pursued his cross-examination:

M.H. – You said one t first, then two; which is it?
Rudrum – I meant two ts.
M.H. – Will you write it down?
Rudrum – I cannot unless you tell me how to spell it. I am a very bad speller.
M.H. – Where did you find the petticoat?
Rudrum – Hanging up by the bed. It was afterwards put in a drawer and not produced again till I was asked for it.
M.H. – Just look at this petticoat. It has been torn or cut after it was marked, because the ink has gone through onto the piece which has been cut off.
Rudrum – Yes.
M.H. – You knew the police were searching everywhere to establish the identity of the woman?
Rudrum – Yes.
M.H. – Do you mean to tell me that the petticoat was hanging up in the woman's room when Lingwood came on 23rd September?
Rudrum – Yes. He saw it I think.
M.H. – Did you not see that he was searching for all the clothes he could find?
Rudrum – You must remember that I was in a very excited state that morning.

At this point the Judge interceded and asked Mrs Rudrum:

> *Can you explain how the petticoat, which was hanging up on a peg in the woman's room, was not discovered on the morning the search was made?*

Rudrum – No my Lord.

With this Marshall Hall seems to have been content that the jury would at least consider the fact that Mrs Rudrum had created this piece of evidence at some point after his client had been charged with the murder.

Marshall Hall was also concerned with Mrs Rudrum's evidence about the watch and link chain as, if it was established that Mrs Hood had owned both of these items, the fact that they were found in Bennett's portmanteau would surely hang his client. The only positive evidence aside from Mrs Rudrum and her daughter's testimony that Mrs Hood had these two items, was the beach photograph taken by a man called Mr Conyers. During Mrs Rudrum's cross-examination she claimed that she was certain that Mrs Hood had been wearing a link chain but was not absolutely sure about the watch. Initially when the police had shown her the chain that they had found in Bennett's portmanteau, she was not sure that it was the same one that she had seen previously.

Rudrum – I was told by the police that they had found the chain.
M.H. – And you believed it, Mrs Rudrum?
Rudrum – No. One does not know what to believe.
M.H. – But you are now prepared to say it was the same chain?
Rudrum – Yes.
M.H. – Are you prepared to back your opinion against your honest doubt. Did you ever realize the meaning of the words, 'I identify the watch and chain produced'?
Rudrum – I never had the chain in my hands.
M.H. – Though you had doubts before, now that you have been cross-examined are you positive?
Rudrum – Yes, I am.
M.H. – Are you equally positive as to the watch?
Rudrum – No.
M.H. – What made you doubt when you first went into the box?
Rudrum – It was the light.
M.H. – But the (beach) photograph has made you certain?
Rudrum – Yes.
M.H. – Are you as sure of that as everything else?
Rudrum – Yes.

Mr Conyers, the beach photographer, had been in the photographic trade for thirty-five years and was shown an enlargement of the snap that he had taken of Mary and Ruby. The first copy was poor but the second he agreed was a reasonable enlargement of the picture that he had taken. He admitted that it was difficult to state whether the chain in the photograph and the actual chain were the same item on account of the fact that the chain in the picture was out of focus. Even Alice Rudrum, when she was cross-examined, agreed that it was not clear from the photograph or from her recollections of having seen the chain whether the item produced in court was one and the same.

When Marshall Hall finally had the opportunity to present his defence case he continually focussed on the fact that many of the witnesses had been given large sums of money by the newspapers for their stories, implying that this had coloured their testimony against his client. However, the main plank of his defence was to try and establish that the watch and chain found in Bennett's portmanteau had nothing to do with the two items that had clearly been taken from the deceased's body. Experts were called to testify that the chain in the photograph was a rope or Prince of Wales design and was nothing like the link chain found in Bennett's lodging room. Marshall Hall also questioned Mrs Cato who told the court that Mrs Bennett actually had two watches and two chains. The one that she was wearing was an imitation gold chain and the one in the photograph could well have been this imitation one. For good measure she also added that Bennett had always treated his wife well.

This time it was Gill's opportunity to destroy one of the witnesses. Mrs Cato had told the *Evening News* that 'Mrs Bennett was a lovable little creature, and if ever a woman was fond of a man she was fond of him. He treated her in a way to crush the love of any woman.' Gill pointed out to the court that her two widely differing views and comments about Bennett were not compatible.

Marshall Hall had an ace up his sleeve in the shape of Douglas Sholto Douglas who was to claim that he had seen Bennett between 6 p.m. and 7 p.m. at Lee Green on 22 September. Douglas described walking back to his house in Hither Green at around 6 p.m. on Saturday, 22nd. A man who asked for a match accosted him; the stranger was wearing a grey suit and a bowler hat and they walked along the road together for a while. The man told Douglas that he worked at the Woolwich Arsenal, had been to Ireland and that he travelled around the country quite a lot. They went into the Tiger public house in Lee Green, Douglas drinking beer and the other man drinking spirits. When they came out of the pub the man pointed to the house next door to the drinking house and told

Douglas that a namesake of his lived there. Douglas could see the nameplate that read 'F K Bennett'. Knowing that Gill would inevitably want to know why Douglas had not come forward until this time, Marshall Hall began to ask the questions himself and started by asking him why he had not come forward until November.

Douglas – About the middle of November I saw the reports of the Yarmouth murder trial.

M.H. – What occurred?

Douglas – Well, when I found that the name of the man charged with the murder was Bennett, when I read of the light grey suit, and that the man worked at Woolwich, I took him for the same man I saw when I was out for a walk on that Saturday, 22nd September. I thought I was justified in making further investigations. I learned afterwards that the prisoner had been in Ireland. All this made me think it was my duty to communicate with the police.

M.H. – Did you see the prisoner?

Douglas – Yes, I went to Norwich and saw him in prison. I did not speak to him nor he to me. I had a good look at him, both full face and profile.

M.H. – And what was your opinion?

Douglas – I had no doubt that the prisoner was the man that I met in the lane on 22nd September.

M.H. – Have you any doubt?

Douglas – I have not a shadow of the doubt about the man or the date.

M.H. – Have you the smallest interest in this case?

Douglas – No. The suggestion is perfectly absurd.

Gill did try to undermine Douglas's evidence but failed to shake him on a single issue. Douglas added that he knew the date was 22 September because he had been potting plants both on 15 September and 29 September as the plants had dates on them. He had no pots with the date 22 September and was, therefore, certain that this was the day that he had encountered the man that he later recognized as Bennett. One has to ask the question why Bennett did not mention the fact that he had had a drink with a man in Lee Green to either the police, his solicitor or defence counsel and that only by chance did Douglas choose to come forward when he did.

Bennett chose not to go into the witness box himself. On the one hand it is claimed that he actually refused to give evidence and on the other that he was considered to be so unreliable that whatever he had said would have put the noose around his own neck. Marshall Hall, in a letter to his friend Sir Arthur Pinero, which was, admittedly, sent after the trial, explained the situation:

> *When I saw that wretched man Bennett on Friday morning alone I said to him this: 'If you will only go into the box and admit everything except the actual murder, I can get a verdict, but of course you must admit that when you saw the papers on the day after the murder you knew it was your wife, but that you were afraid to communicate for fear of losing Alice Meadows'. His reply was: 'I cannot say that, because I was not in Yarmouth on the 22nd, and I never knew that the murdered woman was my wife till I was arrested'. I pointed out that this was hopeless, and he declined to give evidence at all.*

Gill in his summing up told the jury to consider the fact that there was no real answer to where Bennett had been on the nights of the 15 and 22 September. He suggested that Douglas's testimony could have been cobbled together from what had been read in the newspapers.

Marshall Hall's closing statements were interrupted by the arrival of a telegram from Lowestoft. It was from a stationer called O'Driscoll and it read 'Have Lowestoft police made report if not communicate at once most important'. The information was indeed interesting. O'Driscoll said that on Wednesday, 26 September a man had come into his shop in the evening and he saw that the man had scratches on his face and, significantly, one of his boots was laced and the other was not. The man asked O'Driscoll for a newspaper that had a good report on the murder in Great Yarmouth. When the man paid the shopkeeper O'Driscoll also saw that the man's hands were scratched. He added that the man read the newspaper in the shop, groaning whilst he was doing so. The man then became aware that O'Driscoll was staring at him and he had run out of the shop. O'Driscoll relayed all of this evidence in person to a stunned courtroom. Clearly the Lowestoft police had ignored the fact that O'Driscoll had been able to describe the man and the circumstances of his encounter with him. The doctor who had examined Mary's body was recalled and asked whether he had discovered any skin or blood under her fingernails. He had replied in the negative, but had added that the sand may have erased all trace of this.

In the event, Lord Alverstone's summing up was distinctly against Bennett, although he did make a reference to O'Driscoll's testimony and told the jury that 'They ought not to allow such evidence as this to weigh upon their minds if in the end they were satisfied of the guilt of the prisoner'.

With the arguments completed the seven-day trial was at an end and all that now remained was for the jury to consider their verdict. It appears they had little difficulty in making their decision and were back in court in just thirty-five minutes. Inevitably the verdict was guilty. Lord Alverstone had no choice but to don the black cap and pronounce the sentence of death on Herbert John Bennett. He would return to Norfolk for one last time to be hanged in Norwich on 21 March 1901 by James and Thomas Billington. As the black flagstaff was hoisted to signal the impending execution, it snapped which led many to believe in the superstition that Bennett was in fact innocent.

On the face of it much of the evidence seemed overwhelming and, from what the jury saw and heard, the evidence against Bennett was almost conclusive. However, there were too many questions left unanswered. To begin with, why did Bennett choose to stay at the Crown and Anchor Hotel twice, once with Alice Meadows and once on the night that he had murdered his wife? Surely he must have realized that he would have been recognized? Who was the man that the Rudrums claim their Mrs Hood had spoken to and kissed the night before her death? Why would Bennett wish to sexually assault his wife before murdering her on the beach? Where had Bennett's money for all of these trips come from? How had he afforded to support his wife and child and finance his relationship with Alice Meadows? Above all, why did Bennett wait a week before murdering his wife? Every moment that Mary stayed with the Rudrums ran the risk of her revealing to them her real name. And why, in any case, had Mary registered herself with the Rudrums as Mrs Hood? What was Mary doing during the week she spent in Great Yarmouth? Where was she each evening and with whom was she drinking?

It is quite possible that Mary had become involved quite willingly with one of Bennett's scams. It is perfectly possible that Bennett had selected someone against whom to either carry out a fraud or, perhaps blackmail. Perhaps the man that Mary had been seen with on that Friday night was the intended victim. Following this train of thought, the climax of the scam must inevitably have been on Saturday, 22 September. Something inevitably went hopelessly wrong. Even if Mary was involved in some kind of criminal activity with Bennett and that was the purpose of her subterfuge in Great Yarmouth, then it is also reasonable to suspect that Bennett may have intended to have absconded with all of the proceeds of the crime and run off with Alice Meadows anyway.

If we assume that Mary wished to implicate some married or well-connected Great Yarmouth man, then would it not be the perfect thing to be discovered in the act by her husband on the beach at Great Yarmouth? Perhaps the man, sexually pent up after having spent a week with a flirtatious woman, failed to control himself and attempted to sexually assault Mary. In the event, he strangled her and fled the scene. This still leaves many questions unanswered. Were the watch and chain the same as those that the Rudrums claim Mary had worn? More damning, is the fact that Bennett, straight after his wife's death, despite the fact that he had claimed that he was unaware of it, began to make gifts of his wife's possessions to Alice Meadows.

Twelve years after the brutal murder of Mary Bennett another woman was found at virtually the same spot on the South Beach at Great Yarmouth. This time the victim had been strangled with her own bootlace.

Dora May Grey was 18 and lived near the cattle market in Great Yarmouth and worked in a Manby Road boarding house. On 14 July 1912 she had told a friend that she had been to Lowestoft with a gentleman and that she had arranged to meet him again that evening. A witness walking towards South Beach was the last person to see her alive. The only other major difference between this case and the Bennett murder was that it appears that Dora Grey was not actually murdered on the beach and that her body was dragged there by the killer.

Could it be that the same murderer, twelve years after having brutally done away with Mary Bennett, reprised his crime on the unfortunate Dora Grey and that Bennett, after all, was an innocent man? This question remains unsolved.

Finally, as for poor Ruby Bennett, who had lost her mother so tragically in Great Yarmouth and her father on the gallows, she was still only 2 years old and an orphan. Herbert John Bennett's parents willingly adopted their granddaughter and the money received from a newspaper appeal assured her of a comfortable existence into her own adulthood.

CHAPTER 3

Providence House

The murder of Rose Harsent, 1 June 1902

The Peasenhall case has all of the ingredients that a well-crafted work of detective fiction demands. A small, insular village, a host of potential suspects, a series of dark secrets, hypocritical lives, scandal, gossip, a murder and two trials leading to an unsolved mystery. Peasenhall is a relatively small village, with most of the houses on or just off a High Street. It lays to the west of the A12, close to the market town of Halesworth in Suffolk. It provides a truly vintage case at the very end of what could be called the Victorian period.

A drainage ditch and lane, running parallel to the main street in Peasenhall.

One of the houses in this row formerly belonged to William Gardner.

The accused man was William Gardiner. He was highly regarded in his job as a foreman at the Drill Works in the village. He had even represented the business abroad, at the Paris Exhibition. It is fair to say that he was more respected than liked. He was a tall and swarthy man, heavily built, with thick black hair and a full beard. At the time in question, 1901, he was around 34 years old. Gardiner was the father of six children and he was married to Georgina. They lived in a three-bedroom cottage on the High Street, almost in the centre of Peasenhall.

Religion played an important role in the lives of the villagers. Gardiner was a Primitive Methodist elder. He did not attend the local parish church of St Michael but instead his place of worship was no more than a ten-minute walk away, in the Primitive Methodist Chapel on the outskirts of Sibton. The village was not to know that he would be one of two members of the chapel's congregation that would bring scandal and death to the village.

The former Primitive Methodist Chapel in Sibton, where Gardner and Harsent both worshipped.

Gardiner was probably born in around 1867. He had married Georgina Cady from nearby Yoxford in October 1888. About a year or so later they had settled in the village of Peasenhall. In all the couple had had eight children, six of whom had survived. Like most of the workforce in Peasenhall, Gardiner worked for Smythe and Sons, who made farming implements at the Drill Works. He would have been earning around 27s per week. Gardiner was the superintendent, the treasurer, the trustee of the Sunday school, the Assistant Society Steward and the choirmaster for the Primitive Methodist community. It was to be his association with the choir that would bring about his downfall, as one of the choristers was Rose Harsent.

Rose Anne Harsent was around 22 years old in 1901, a full twelve years younger than Gardiner. There is some confusion as to her father, who would later play an important role in the case.

His job is variously described as either being someone who delivered milk to farms, or that he worked as a carter at the Drill Works. In either case, central to the story is Rose herself and her relationship with the Primitive Methodists.

Deacon Crisp employed Rose. He was a prominent member of the local chapel. The Deacon and his wife were fairly elderly and Rose was employed as a domestic servant. Rose had, in fact, replaced a girl that had been dismissed about three years earlier after she had fallen pregnant. The Crisps' home was called Providence House.

As William Henderson, in *The Notable British Trials* described Rose:

> *Living as she did in a part of England not notably celebrated for a particularly high standard of moral purity, she was probably a fair specimen of the girlhood of her district.*

Rose certainly had several admirers, although the only surviving photograph of her does not paint a picture of an English rose, but more a plain and ordinary looking girl. As Henderson wrote:

A view of the side of Providence House.

[Rose] *had not been altogether free from certain gross accompaniments* [and that] *the cruder side of her amorous adventures was not entirely distasteful to her.*

Providence House is a rambling building and at the time it was rather ramshackle. Rose's bedroom was over the kitchen and could be reached by a flight of stairs that led from the kitchen. Her room was not, therefore, easily accessible from the rest of the building. In effect we could think of the kitchen, in which Rose generally worked, and her bedroom above it to be something like an adjoining cottage to the rest of the house. The Crisps were very religious people and it seems that they were kind and caring towards Rose.

Before her murder and, indeed, afterwards during the trial, there was considerable debate about her immorality. Mrs Crisp was asked at the trial, by the defence counsel: 'If you believed this girl was an immoral young woman, would you not have kept her?'

To which the reply was 'No I should not'.

In fact it was this very question of immorality that would lead to Rose's death and to the most serious allegations being laid against Gardiner.

The Doctor's Chapel.

The rumour and innuendos had begun on 1 May 1901. Georgina Gardiner was heavily pregnant and expected to give birth very soon. On that evening Rose was seen to enter a small, thatched building, called the Doctor's Chapel. Rose's employer, William Crisp, who was a retired tailor, was deacon of the Doctor's Chapel. One of Rose's duties was, therefore, to sweep and clean the tiny chapel every week. The Doctor's Chapel was away from the main road, close to the Drill Works. It took only a minute or so to walk there from Providence House.

Two young men, George Wright, who was known in the village as Bill, and Alphonso Skinner, who was known as Fonzo, saw Rose going into the Doctor's Chapel. They then saw Gardiner follow her in. They were intrigued and crept towards the Doctor's Chapel and eavesdropped on the conversation. They heard what they later claimed was sexual activity and laughter. By all accounts neither Bill nor Fonzo were particularly nice young men. Bill was around 22 years old and Fonzo was a little older. As they worked with Gardiner at the Drill Works they were used to his sanctimonious behaviour, but now they had witnessed his lust. They lost little time in spreading the gossip around the village.

It clearly caused Gardiner a great deal of difficulty, not to mention embarrassment. Gardiner absolutely denied what had happened and even when a circuit superintendent of the Primitive Methodists came to investigate, he flatly denied the accusations.

On 8 May Gardiner called for Bill and Fonzo to come and see him and demanded that they give him a written apology. The two youths refused. On 11 May the senior Primitive Methodists gathered in Sibton, under the chairmanship of the Reverend John Guy. Also in attendance was a lay preacher called Rouse. They carefully considered the testimony of Bill and Fonzo then listened to Gardiner. They did not call Rose.

It was Guy's opinion that the tale was fabricated and, in any case, Bill and Fonzo were Church of England worshippers; much less trustworthy than Gardiner, the Primitive Methodist. Beyond any doubt the whole investigation was designed to bury the scandal.

Gardiner resigned all of his offices but was immediately re-elected to all of them. Guy took Rose aside and assured her that they did not believe that she had had an illicit relationship with Gardiner. Gardiner was also warned not to be too friendly with the women in the choir.

There were two letters that passed between Gardiner and Rose between 8 and 11 May. What is of particular interest is that Rose chose not to destroy them. They were found in her possessions after her death and in many respects it was these two letters that would bring Gardiner to court.

The first letter said:

Dear Rose,

I was very much surprised this morning to hear there's some scandal going the round about you and me going into the Doctor's Chapel for immoral purposes so that I shall put it into other hands at once as I have found out who it was that started it. Bill Wright and Skinner say they saw us there but I shall summons them for deformation of character unless they withdraw what they have said and give me an apology. I shall see Bob tonight and we will come and see you together if possible. I shall at the same time see your father and tell him.

William Gardiner signed this.

One question that has never quite been answered is the identity of Bob. There were no witnesses at the trial with that Christian name and although there was some suggestion that Bob was one of Rose's brothers, this is not the Bob that was referred to in the letter.

For some reason the meeting did not go ahead with Rose, Gardiner and Bob. So Gardiner wrote a second letter:

Dear Rose,

I have broke the news to Mrs Gardiner this morning, she is awfully upset but she say she know it is wrong for I was at home from half past nine o'clock so I could not possibly be with you an hour so she won't believe anything about it. I have asked Mr Burgess to ask those too Chaps to come to the chapel tonight and have it out there however they stand by such a tale I don't know but I don't think God will forsake me now and if we put our trust in Him it will end right but its awfully hard work to have to face people when they are all suspicious of you but by God's help whether they believe me or not I shall try to live it down and prove by my future conduct that it's all false, I only wish I could take it to Court but I don't see a shadow of a chance to get the case as I don't think you'll be strong

*enough to face a trial. Trusting that God will direct us and
make the way clear, I remains yours in trouble W. Gardiner.*

Gardiner had, in fact, consulted a solicitor. Whatever the
strength of his case against Bill and Fonzo, it was unlikely that
Gardiner would ever recover his costs. The two men were
virtually penniless, but the solicitor did write to them,
threatening that legal proceeding would begin unless they
apologized within seven days. They did not respond and
officially the matter dropped there. What is clear, however, is
that the gossiping did not stop and probably neither did the
relationship between Gardiner and Rose. They were meeting on
a regular basis, certainly during choir practice and during the
Sunday services.

It also seems that Mrs Crisp had words with Rose on the
scandal. Rose had denied the story in an emphatic manner and
Mrs Crisp seemed to believe her. The one person that took the
least notice of the gossip was Georgina, Gardiner's wife. She
was devoted to her husband and had faith in him. She was
quoted as saying:

*I have a good husband. All this talk about him and Rosie does
not trouble me because I know it's not true.*

In due course the gossip began to subside and it may have been
the case that Rose had taken another lover, a shop assistant at
Emmett's Store in Peasenhall. He was desperately in love with
her and he wrote her many love letters:

*My innermost yearnings have made me write down on paper
a few lines about her who has enraptured my heart, a rose
among the many thorns that reside in our midst. Her shapely
form and wavy hair make her the idol that I worship, she
means to me my very existence. A glimpse of her will cheer me
at any time throughout the day. The time may come when she
will leave me to woo some other man, then life will not be
worth living, but should I win her heart for my own it will be
like heaven on earth. Like the old song, she's a lily of the valley
and the bright and morning star.*

This was, perhaps, one of the most poetic of the letters that had
been written to Rose. Many of the others were frankly smutty
and full of innuendo.

Emmett's Store in Peasenhall.

About nine months after the original scandal about Gardiner and Rose, Henry Rouse saw them walking down a lane together at nine in the evening. A few days later Rouse confronted Gardiner and told him he could 'do the chapel a great deal of harm'. Gardiner would later completely deny that this conversation had ever taken place.

About a month later, whilst Rouse was delivering a sermon in the chapel, he saw Gardiner's feet resting on Rose's lap. He would later recount this in court:

You gentlemen know what I mean by the lap of a person. I ceased to speak, with the intention of telling one of them to walk out of the chapel but something seemed to speak to me not to expose them there.

In fact he did not mention this to anyone and dictated a letter to be written by his wife on 14 April 1902. It was to be sent anonymously to Gardiner:

Mr Gardiner,

I write to warn you of your conduct with that girl Rose, I find when she come into the chapel she must place herself next to you, which keep the peoples' minds still in the belief that you are a guilty man, and in that case you will drive many from the chapel, and those that will join the cause are kept away through it. We are told to shun the least appearance of evil. I do not wish you to leave God's house, but there must be a difference before God's cause can prosper, which I hope you will see to be right as people cannot hear when the enemy of souls bring this before them. I write to you as one that love your soul, and I hope you will have her sit in some other place and remove such feeling which for sake she will do.

By this stage Rose was pregnant. She had borrowed a book on abortion. Her condition was even obvious to Mrs Crisp. If the gossips could be believed there was a married, respectable, chapel-going man in Peasenhall whose illegitimate child was being carried by Rose.

On the afternoon of Saturday, 31 May 1902 a postman called Brewer delivered a letter in a yellow envelope to Providence House. As it would be later pointed out, the yellow envelope was very similar to the ones used by the offices at the Drill Works. The postmark showed that it had been posted the same day in a neighbouring village. The letter read:

Dear R

I will try to see you tonight at 12 o'clock at your place. If you put a light in your window at 10 for about 10 minutes then you can put it out again. Do not have a light in your room at 12, as I will come round the back way.

The letter was unsigned, so it was clear that whoever had written it was known to Rose and that she would understand its message.

On the night of 31 May 1902 there was a dramatic thunderstorm. There was heavy rain and the roads were thick with mud. As Mrs Crisp would later say, she was concerned about Rose sleeping in her isolated bedroom at the other end of the house. She said to her husband 'I think I'd better get up and see if Rose is frightened'. Deacon Crisp was of the opinion that Rose would not be frightened and that his wife should stay in bed. Mrs Crisp could not sleep and just before the church clock struck 12 she heard what she thought was breaking glass and a muffled scream.

Gardiner had been standing by his front door, watching the storm. He, like Henry Burgess, who was also about, could have seen the light gleaming from the top window of Providence House. After all it was only a couple of hundred yards up the road. Later that night Rosanna Dickenson, the Gardiners' next-door neighbour, came into the Gardiners' house to keep Georgina company, while the storm was raging. As they would later testify, William Gardiner was with them.

The morning brought a still day and Rose's father, William, was approaching Providence House at around eight o'clock in the morning. Some accounts say that he was bringing milk. Whatever the case, he always used the opportunity to take Rose a change of clothes and freshly laundered underwear. He knocked at the back door and there was no reply. He automatically thought that his daughter had been kept awake by the storm and she was still asleep, so he knocked more loudly. There was still no reply. Then something made him look through the window into the kitchen. The sight chilled his heart, for lying on the floor in her nightdress and stockings was his daughter.

William opened the back door. The room was only 10 feet 6 inches by 8 feet 6 inches and the body was turned towards the wall. Some paraffin had been spilled on the floor and some newspaper had been placed under the body. There had been some attempt to set fire to Rose. This had only managed to burn part of her nightdress and charred her arms and the lower part of her body. This was not, however, the cause of death. Later, as a medical expert would state, there had been an upward thrust into the chest and there were two slashes across her throat, which had severed the windpipe and cut her neck from ear to ear. There were spurts of blood between her head and the wall. There were no signs of footprints. It appeared that William's daughter had been killed literally as she had left the staircase coming down into the kitchen.

William pulled a rug over his daughter's body and moved nothing from the scene, apart from the metal top of a broken paraffin lamp. He stumbled outside, distraught. When just outside he met James Crisp, who was making an early call to his brother's house. James Crisp looked inside the kitchen and the pair of them decided that they needed to get help immediately.

The news travelled quickly and soon the village constable, Eli Nun, arrived. It was about twenty minutes to nine.

A doctor was sent for and Nun made an initial investigation of the murder scene. It appeared that Rose had been carrying the lamp in her hand and then had dropped it. There was a broken medicine bottle, which had a label that said 'for Mrs Gardiner's children'. The fire had been started by the 30 May edition of the *East Anglian Daily Times*. This was not the Crisps' newspaper, but it was one that was taken by Gardiner. It was Nun's original belief that this was a case of suicide. It was also abundantly clear that Rose was heavily pregnant.

The police searched Rose's bedroom, where they found Gardiner's two letters and also the third note, which had been delivered to Rose only the day before. The initial thought was that the handwriting was the same.

Meanwhile, Gardiner had left his home at nine o'clock in the

The front of Providence House. Rose Harsent's room is obscured by the tree to the far right of the building.

morning to take his children to Sunday school. He was not made aware of the death of Rose for another two hours. When he was told he showed no sign of surprise.

On the following Monday morning the case was handed over to Superintendent Staunton. Staunton first questioned Gardiner that morning. He was asked whether he had written the last letter; Gardiner denied it but admitted that the handwriting did look like his own. Staunton realized that there was more information that Gardiner needed to tell him, but other information had also been coming to light.

At ten o'clock on the Saturday evening, whilst the storm had been in full spate, Burgess, the local bricklayer, had talked to Gardiner for about a quarter of an hour. He confirmed that he had seen the light at the top of Providence House. If he had seen it Burgess believed that Gardiner had positioned himself by his front door so that he also had a clear view.

On Tuesday evening after the killing, the coroner opened the investigations and Gardiner found himself charged with the murder of Rose Harsent. The trouble was that Gardiner could account for virtually every minute of his time. There was to be other damning evidence that would come to light that would begin to cast doubt on whether Gardiner was telling the truth.

A gamekeeper called James Morriss had been walking along Peasenhall High Street at five o'clock on the Sunday morning. He claimed to have clearly seen in the mud a single set of footprints leaving Gardiner's house towards Providence House and then back again.

One of the jurors in the inquest drew a blank sole on a piece of paper and Morriss was asked to draw the sole marks. He drew two parallel bars across it. The police had already collected most of Gardiner's clothing, but they could not match any of his footwear with the sole marks. On 6 June the police called on Georgina Gardiner and asked her whether her husband had any India rubber soled shoes. She produced a pair that had been given to her by her brother just the week before the murder. The sole marks were identical to those the gamekeeper had drawn.

There were some other confusing bits of evidence. As far as Mrs Crisp was concerned, she thought she had heard the scream between one and two o'clock, but it may have been around midnight. Rose was expecting a visitor at midnight. Rose's bed had not been slept in; presumably she had waited up to let her visitor in.

Handwriting experts also pointed the finger of blame at

Gardiner. But as for the bloodstains, there was nothing conclusive. There were no bloodstains on Gardiner's clothing, but his penknife was rather more interesting. The knife had been recently sharpened and it had been scraped inside. However there was still some residual blood inside the hinge. In a time before blood could be analysed, all the police expert could be sure about was that it was mammal's blood and that it was probably less than a month old. Gardiner claimed it was rabbit's blood and that he had used the knife to disembowel rabbits.

The police had also found a small piece of woollen material beside Rose's body. But this could not be matched to any clothing owned by Gardiner. The envelope containing the last letter to Rose was more interesting. But again lacking the technology to analyse it for fingerprints or for DNA, the police had no way of knowing whether it was sent by Gardiner using stationery from the Drill Works or whether it had been sent by a third party and the choice of envelope was purely coincidental.

There was, however, enough circumstantial evidence to send Gardiner to trial. The police would have to rely on motive and for that they would have to rely on Bill and Fonzo. In order to check their story Burgess, Bill and Fonzo accompanied Constable Nun to the Doctor's Chapel on 28 July. Nun wanted to re-enact what had happened and find out whether it was possible to hear anything. It was Nun's opinion that it was perfectly possible that they had heard what they claimed.

Shortly before the case at Ipswich Assizes, the police unearthed another potentially damning piece of circumstantial evidence. Herbert Stammers' house overlooked the yard behind Gardiner's house. He claimed that around half past seven on that Sunday morning he had seen Gardiner go into the washhouse. Gardiner had lit a fire inside and the inference was that he had destroyed his bloodstained clothing. Circumstantially it worked as an idea, because the police had only found two of Gardiner's shirts.

Gardiner's trial opened at Ipswich Assizes on 7 November 1902. The judge was Mr Justice Grantham; the son of Charles Dickens, Mr Henry F. Dickens, and later Sir Henry Dickens QC, handled the prosecution. The Honourable John De Grey supported him. Representing Gardiner was Sir Ernest Wild and Mr Claughton Scott. The case for good or ill would establish the reputation of the great defender, Wild.

In the first trial the defence clearly hung on the fact that both Gardiner and his wife Georgina testified in the witness box that they were in the company of a neighbour until midnight. After that they were in bed together until eight o'clock the following morning. Gardiner emphatically denied writing the last note and stated that he had not worn the pair of India rubber soled shoes. Under cross-examination Gardiner refused to be budged.

The jury retired to consider their verdict at 1615 on the last day and did not return until 2040. What is particularly interesting is the exchange between Mr Justice Grantham and the foreman of the jury. It certainly suggests that the judge was of the opinion that Gardiner was a guilty man:

Grantham – Are you agreed upon your verdict?
Foreman – No my lord. I don't know whether you can help us in any way?
Grantham – Is there any assistance I can give you in answering any questions?

The reply was no.

Grantham – There is no prospect of you agreeing?
Foreman – I'm afraid not, my lord. You don't wish to know our position?
Grantham – Well, one gentleman says he does not want to ask any questions. I suppose he is the one who does not agree, and has intimated that there is no chance of his agreeing. You have said you don't wish to ask any questions. Do you think time may be of any value to you in considering the question?
One of the jurors – I have not made up my mind not to agree if I was convinced that the prisoner was guilty, but I have heard nothing to convince me that he is guilty.
Grantham – I have no doubt that everything has been said, and if it has not convinced you, I do not think it is any good keeping the jury any longer at great inconvenience. I think there is only one thing to do. I am extremely sorry, but that is to discharge you without giving a verdict.

There was nothing for it but for Gardiner to be tried again. In the meantime the Peasenhall villagers were unpleasant and cruel to Georgina. Her husband was in prison and she had money problems. She had to beg for cash to pay for her husband's defence and to support her and the children. Her eldest child was only 13 years old.

The new judge was the Honourable Sir John Compton Lawrence. He was a former Member of Parliament, had once been the recorder of Derby, the leader of the Midlands Circuit and he had served as a judge for twelve years. The trial at County Hall in Ipswich drew an enormous crowd. It opened on Wednesday, 21 January 1903.

Gardiner appeared in a sombre black suit, betraying little in the way of emotion throughout the entire trial. One of the major problems for both the prosecution and for the defence was the fact that this was not only a well publicized trial, but it had also ended in a previous stalemate just a couple of months before.

Dickens, prosecuting, made an attempt to urge the jury not to take anything else into account barring the evidence that they were about to hear. He began his introduction by describing the key parts of the case. He referred to the layout of Providence House and the fact that the murder had taken place in a relatively isolated part of the building. He also referred to the alleged activities in the Doctor's Chapel and the evidence that would be provided by Bill and Fonzo. Dickens also speculated about the oil lamp and the broken medicine bottle. It was Dickens' contention that the murderer had brought the medicine bottle full of paraffin to start a fire. Unfortunately for the murderer the cork had been pushed into the bottle too hard and deep so he was unable to open it. Instead he dismantled the oil lamp, but again could not gain access to the paraffin. Crucially, Dickens claimed that the murderer, in his eyes Gardiner, had then smashed the medicine bottle onto the floor, forgetting that his name was on the label.

There has always been conjecture about this particular theory. One contemporary newspaper was right in its suggestion that the paraffin and the newspaper were never sufficient to set fire to the body of Rose Harsent as it lay in the kitchen. Their theory was that the murderer had intended to kill Rose Harsent in her bed and then use the paraffin and the newspaper to start the fire. The bed would have burst into flames and destroyed Rose Harsent's body. Their theory was that when the murder took place in the kitchen, rather than Rose's bedroom the murderer panicked. After all we know that Mrs Crisp believed that she had heard screams during the night. The murderer had to shut Rose up quickly and perhaps did not have the time nor the nerve to carry the victim up the staircase, place her in bed and then set fire to the body.

Dickens was particularly keen, after his summary of the

evidence, to provide a motive for the murder. He told the jury:

> *Then there is the girl in the family way – six months gone.*
> *Someone in Peasenhall must have had an interest in getting*
> *rid of the girl, because no one can suggest that this murder was*
> *committed for gain or for robbery or for jealousy. It was for the*
> *object of getting rid of the girl, and if possible of destroying the*
> *body.*

This was at the heart of the entire case. Given that an attempt
had been made to set fire to the body it presumed one of two
things, although they could be connected. Firstly the
destruction of the body would hide the means by which the
murder had been committed. There would be no evidence of
slashes or stab wounds. The second showed even more premed-
itation. If the body was consumed by fire then it would be
impossible for anyone to tell that Rose had been pregnant at the
time of her murder. Thereby, as Dickens suggested, the
principle motive for the murder would be concealed.

The first key witnesses were, of course, George Wright and
Alphonso Skinner. Unsurprisingly they corroborated one
another's evidence. They clearly described precisely what had
happened in the Doctor's Chapel. Under cross-examination
Wright was accused by Wild that he had made up the story
of the Doctor's Chapel incident because Gardiner had
reprimanded him at work and it was purely a question of
revenge. Wright had obviously been working this out himself
and at least someone had predicted for him that this could be a
line of questioning. He was sure that Gardiner had reprimanded
him at work after the chapel incident. He also told the court that
he actually felt grateful to Gardiner because he had been instru-
mental in gaining him promotion to become a wheelwright.

Wild had also dug up something else on Wright, an incident
that had happened possibly five to seven years beforehand.
Wright and some friends had climbed a tree so that they could
spy on a man called Cady and his girlfriend in an orchard.
Interesting to relate the fact that Cady was probably a brother-
in-law of Gardiner, as Georgina's maiden name was Cady.

Next came the turn of Skinner to be cross-examined. Wild
claimed that he had learned his story off by heart. After all he
had told it several times, to the elders of the chapel, to the
coroner, to the magistrates and in the first trial. When he was
pressed by Wild he told the court that originally Gardiner had

denied ever going to the Doctor's Chapel with Rose and then had admitted he had, but that nothing had happened.

The Reverend John Guy was the next witness. He became angry when he was taken to task that he had once said that the elders of the chapel had actually questioned Rose Harsent. Wild even went on to suggest that Guy's testimony should be struck off because he had a defective memory. It became clear from Guy's evidence that he did think that there was something behind the accusations against Gardiner in regard of his relationship with Rose. Wild also turned up evidence about Guy's past. Guy had found himself in a very similar position to Gardiner some time before.

Henry Rouse now appeared. By this stage he was 73 years old and had been involved with the Primitive Methodist Chapel for thirty-five years. He was a labourer and a lay preacher. He had the appearance of being a very pious, self-righteous and rather vindictive man. He told the court he had continued to watch Gardiner after the enquiry into the Doctor's Chapel incident. He had confronted Gardiner on one occasion when he had seen him walking with Rose. Wild took him to task about the anonymous letter, which Rouse had to finally admit that he had dictated to his wife.

Wild then rounded on Rouse with information aimed to discredit him. The first piece of evidence tried to show that Rouse had a history of unsubstantiated accusations. He had brought a charge of arson against a 13 year old boy, a case that was dismissed by magistrates. Rouse had also been accused of misconduct with the wife of a farmer. Wild claimed that Rouse had visited the woman, pretending to be spreading the gospel. But in fact he had called on her for completely different reasons. There was another similar accusation, which had caused Rouse to move away from the district. He quarrelled with neighbours and when he fell out with a village over money, he told the village's vicar that the man's daughters were prostitutes. Rouse denied everything but Wild had done the damage and this had very much undermined Rouse's evidence.

Harry Harsent appeared next. He was the 14 year old brother of Rose. He told the court that he had taken letters between Gardiner and Rose on several occasions between 1901 and 1902. This was slightly different evidence to the statements that he had made in the first trial, when he had said that he had not taken any letters in 1902. In fact Gardiner had admitted to writing to Rose twice and she had clearly written to him once;

that was related to hymn choices for choir practice.

The last person to appear on the first day was Mrs Crisp. She was confused as to the time when she had heard the scream and could only estimate that it was some time between one and two in the morning. Under cross-examination Wild called her a liar. If it could have been firmly established when Mrs Crisp had heard the scream then a presumed time of death could have been established. It would then have been a simple case of showing whether Gardiner had had the opportunity to be in Providence House at that time.

Interestingly, neither the prosecution nor the defence called Deacon Crisp, who may or may not have been able to shed some light on the timing of the scream.

On the second day of the trial there was police and medical evidence. To begin with Burgess testified that he had seen Gardiner standing on his doorstep at around ten o'clock. Rosanna Dickenson, Gardiner's next-door neighbour confirmed that she and Georgina Gardiner had been together until about 2330. By midnight William Gardiner had joined them and they were together until 0130. Dickens made the inference that Gardiner could have committed the crime before he had joined Mrs Dickenson and Georgina. The other inference, of course, was that Gardiner had originally claimed that he and his wife had been with Mrs Dickenson all of the time.

An unfortunate comparison was made with the next witness, Morriss. He, it will be recalled, was a gamekeeper. Morriss had claimed that he had seen footprints between Gardiner's house and Providence House. What was particularly interesting about this evidence was that he had seen these footprints much later and had Gardiner committed the crime before he had joined his wife and Mrs Dickenson, the footprints would have been washed away by the rain.

The next witness was Stammers, Gardiner's next-door neighbour. He was tackled by Wild with regard to the evidence that he had given in the first trial. Wild contended that Stammers had been induced by the original judge to state that Gardiner had set a large fire. Originally Stammers had described it as simply a fire. All Stammers could add to his testimony was that in the twelve or so months that he had been a neighbour to the Gardiners he had never seen them light a fire in the washhouse on a Sunday morning.

John Samuel Rickards dealt with the question of the envelopes and Gardiner's handwriting. Comparisons were made, but it was not absolutely clear whether the handwriting was the same, particularly when they compared Wright's reprimand, written by Gardiner, and other samples of Gardiner's handwriting. The question about the envelopes was also unresolved; they were common and cost around 3s for a thousand.

Eli Nun, the village constable, now gave his testimony. He described how he had found the body; it was lying on its side with burns on the body and on the nightdress. He described a burnt out candle, a broken bottle with the label and a smashed paraffin lamp. He also described collecting Gardiner's clothes, telling the court that he found that Gardiner only owned two shirts. The judge would refer to this matter in his summing up and said:

> *The accused had a clean shirt on that morning, and how, after a fortnight's wear, that could be managed, I do not know.*

In fact Gardiner's other shirt was dirty, so it can be presumed that he had just changed his shirt. Mrs Gardiner would later confirm that she did the washing every fortnight.

When Wild cross-examined Nun he began by concentrating on the acoustic tests that he had carried out at the Doctor's Chapel. Wild claimed that no inference could be drawn from Nun's tests. Nun admitted under cross-examination that when he had first seen Rose's body he thought it was suicide:

> *I did not think of anything else. Of course after seeing the wounds and finding the letter it made me think of something else.*

Nun was, of course, referring to the letter of assignation that had been sent to Rose the day before she was killed. Nun also passed comment on the other letters and could confirm that some of them had been sent to her by Frederick Davis, Rose's next-door neighbour.

Wild also attacked Nun about his interviewing Mrs Gardiner while her husband was under suspicion. It was Nun's opinion that the best course of action was to prevent the Gardiners from getting together and concocting a story.

The next person in the witness box was Superintendent Staunton. He confirmed that the only major difference between the statements made by Gardiner and Mrs Gardiner was whether they had been together all of the time with Mrs

Dickenson. Under cross-examination Staunton admitted that he had agreed with Nun's first inclination about Rose and that it was probably a suicide.

Mr Wild also asked Superintendent Staunton about three confessions, which he had received about the murder of Rose. One of the letters had come from a man called Goodchild, who was a brewer and there had been a sizeable investigation into whether this man had been involved in the murder. In the end there was no chance that he could have been in the right place to send the assignation letter. The other two confessions seem to have come from lunatics.

The medical evidence came next; firstly, Dr Charles Ryder Richardson, who had carried out the post mortem. He was able to describe the wounds to Rose's neck and the wound that had virtually severed her windpipe:

> *There were numerous semi-circular cuts about her hands, most of which were caused by upward blows such as in warding off blows.*

This testimony alone seemed to infer that suicide was not an option and that Rose had definitely been attacked.

Dr Charles Edward Lay had made a preliminary examination of Rose's body on the Sunday morning. He believed that she had died around four hours before the body was discovered. This would have put the time of death, given the time delay in calling the doctor, at something like 4 to 5 a.m. on the Sunday morning. This would seem to infer that the only window of opportunity that Gardiner might have had to have murdered Rose was four or more hours earlier than this.

Dr Stevenson, the Senior Home Office Analyst, now told the court that his investigations had centred on trying to find any sign of blood or paraffin on Gardiner's clothing. What he had found was blood between the handle and the blade of Gardiner's penknife. In his own words, he found the knife's condition to be rather odd:

> *It was a little oily and had evidently been freshly cleaned and sharpened. It had been scraped inside the haft. On examining the interior of the handle and between the metal and bone of the handle I found a minute quantity of mammalian blood. I should say that the blood inside had not been more than a month there.*

Stevenson also gave evidence about the medicine bottle that was alleged to have contained paraffin. He was of the opinion that the cork had been forced deep into the neck so that it would have been impossible to prize it out using fingers. The broken bottle had been fractured in Stevenson's view by the heat.

Wild asked Dr Stevenson about a minute piece of cloth that had been found at the scene. He asked Stevenson where he had found it:

> *It had dropped out of the paper containing the glass, which was in a small box. I did not find it during my first examination, but a day or two after when it turned out amongst the debris of the bottle.*

Frederick Davis was now called to the witness box. He was taken to task about the letters he had written to Rose. There was no real inference by anyone that Davis had done anything worse than writing dirty letters to Rose. Whilst Davis was clearly embarrassed in having his letters read out in court, they did not really prove anything one way or the other.

The prosecution's trump card was their last witness, Thomas Gurrin, who was a handwriting expert. The prosecution asked him whether it was his opinion that the samples of business letters written by Gardiner matched the assignation letter written to Rose. Gurrin answered:

> *To the best of my belief these documents that I have been comparing were all written by the same hand.*

Under Wild's cross-examination Gurrin admitted that he had some reservations and that handwriting analysis could be imprecise.

Wild began his defence of Gardiner on Friday, 23 January 1903. At this stage Gardiner had been in prison on remand for 234 days. Wild said that Gardiner was:

> *Perhaps not too popular owing to the fact that he is a teetotaller, and that he is a man professing religion.*

Wild urged the jury to find his client:

> *Not guilty of the atrocious charge which had unjustly been brought against him.*

Wild pointed out that Gardiner had been cleared of the scandal regarding the Doctor's Chapel. He contended that even if the jury believed that Gardiner had written the assignation letter this did not mean he was a murderer. He promised that Gardiner would explain how the bottle with his name on it had ended up in Providence House, why there was blood on his penknife, why Morriss's evidence was wrong and how Stammers had exaggerated the size of the fire. Wild also pointed out that it would have been impossible for Gardiner to have committed the murder and leave no trace of blood or paraffin on his clothes or scratches to his body.

Wild's first witness was Georgina Gardiner. She was convinced of her husband's innocence and could recall precisely all of the events eight months earlier when the murder had taken place over the weekend. Mrs Gardiner said that she and her husband had kept company with Mrs Dickenson from between 2300 and 2330 on the Saturday evening, until around 0130 on the Sunday morning. The only time that her husband had not been with her was when he had gone to make sure that their children were safely tucked up in bed.

Georgina explained very clearly as to why the medicine bottle with the Gardiners' name on it was found in Providence House. Some time ago the medicine bottle had contained a draft for one of the children. After it was empty she used it to buy camphorated oil. On an occasion in the past Rose Harsent had complained that she had a chest cold. Mrs Gardiner had given her the bottle and it was this series of events that accounted for its presence at the murder scene. She also said that the newspaper that had been found under Rose's body was not the copy that had been delivered to Gardiner's house. In fact she could not find it and believed that it had been destroyed. Further she was certain that her husband was reading it on the Sunday morning, as he usually did.

She was obviously a very scared woman, as she fainted shortly before she was cross-examined.

As Henderson wrote:

> *There had been much cruel suspense connected with the case, but a belief in her husband's innocence might have been expected to inspire her with greater fortitude, unless of course she was in weak health or abnormally temperamental.*

Georgina claimed that the fire had been set on the Sunday

morning to boil a kettle. She claimed that Stammers, Rouse, Wright and Skinner were liars and that Morriss was simply mistaken. She also confirmed that Gardiner only owned two shirts and that he changed his shirt every Sunday.

Gardiner now appeared in the witness box. He described the events of 1 May 1901, completely denying the version of events given by Wright and Skinner. He recounted to the court that he had confronted them and he also spoke about the enquiry that had taken place in the chapel. He explained that letters that had passed between himself and Rose related to chapel matters and that the blood that had been found on his knife could be put down to the disembowelling and skinning of rabbits.

Evidence now moved to 31 May 1902. Gardiner explained his movements from the time he came home from work on Saturday evening to the point where he took his children to Sunday school the following morning. Gardiner explained that he had gone to bed around two in the morning, about half an hour after parting company with Mrs Dickenson. His wife had got up twice in the night, first to comfort their son Bertie, who had been awoken by the storm and the second time to get some brandy to calm a stomach ache. He had not got out of bed until 0800 on the Sunday morning.

Under cross-examination Dickens asked him:

'Had you any knowledge whatever of the death of Rose Harsent until you heard of it in going to Sunday school?'

Gardiner categorically stated that he had not.

Dickens was equally concerned with the allegations regarding the Doctor's Chapel back in 1901 and asked Gardiner:

'Now we come to Rouse. Is Mr Rouse's story a fabrication from beginning to end?'

Gardiner said that it was. But Dickens pressed him: 'Not a word of truth in it?'

Again Gardiner replied no.

Dickens tried one last time: 'Is it untrue that you were walking with a girl late at night?'

Again Gardiner said that this was not the truth.

Dickens was seeking a gap in Gardiner's armour and now turned to the chapel enquiry and the conversation he had had with John Guy afterwards: 'Is it true you told Mr Guy you would keep clear of young women generally, and of Rose Harsent in particular?'

Gardiner replied: 'No I did not'.

Dickens asked: 'Anything of that kind?'

'No, because I had no reason to keep clear of Rose Harsent' was the reply.

Dickens wondered whether Gardiner had a reason for believing that Wright and Skinner should make up stories about him: 'Can you suggest any ill feeling in either of these two boys against you?'

Gardiner replied: 'Not until this scandal, and then they were forced to stick to it, and there has been ill feeling ever since, and there always will continue to be.'

Gardiner was interestingly defensive about Rose when Dickens asked him: 'With regard to Rose Harsent, you never saw her guilty of any impropriety of conduct?'

Gardiner replied: 'I cannot say I have never seen her walking with anyone, but I can say this, I have never seen anything improper between her and other men.'

Following Gardiner was a number of defence witnesses, whose testimony was aimed to discredit the prosecution evidence. A pair of senior bank officials called James Fairbank and Herbert Bayliss countered the evidence that had been given by Gurrin. Several elders from the Primitive Methodist Chapel attested to the good character of Gardiner.

Georgina's fainting had put off the cross-examination, but there was no way of avoiding it now. It was the fourth and final day of the trial and Mrs Gardiner now found herself facing a determined cross-examination by Dickens. The interchange between the pair was as follows:

Dickens – What time did you suggest you went to Mrs Dickenson's that night?
Georgina – About half past eleven, I should say.
Dickens – Am I right in saying you told the police 'we went at 11 and stopped till half past 1?'
Georgina – I did not say to the police the exact time. I told them my husband came shortly after, the same as I told you when I gave my evidence at the last trial.
Dickens – Half an hour afterwards?
Georgina – No, a very few minutes after.
Dickens – Do you mean he almost followed you in?
Georgina – I told you what he did. He went upstairs to look at the children.

Dickens was still trying to put forward the theory that Gardiner had had the opportunity to leave the house, go to Providence House, kill Rose and return. He had around half an hour to do this. Dickens now tried to see whether he could ascertain Georgina's view of Rose Harsent:

Dickens – Rose Harsent of course was constantly at your house?
Georgina – Not constantly she came when she liked.
Dickens – You never saw her guilty of impropriety with any man?
Georgina – No.
Dickens – Of course, if your husband had walked out with her, you did not know it?
Georgina – My husband never did walk out with her.
Dickens –You cannot say that, but of course you believe in your husband?
Georgina –Yes, I do.

The trial now moved to its final stage, with the summing up of the prosecution and the defence and, of course, the all-important judge's summing up.

Wild used every trick in the book, trying to play on the jury's emotions by saying: 'Are these poor helpless children to be branded for all time as the children of a man who has committed such a dastardly crime?'

On the flimsiest of evidence Wild suggested that Frederick Davis was the father of Rose's unborn child. He had of course absolutely nothing to support this view. Wild also pointed out that if Gardiner was guilty of the murder then his wife was an accomplice, by both her support and her testimony. In Wild's view the scandal of 1901 was over and done with, thus discounting anything that was said by Wright, Skinner and Rouse. He also pointed out that his own experts had refuted Gurrin's evidence. Wild pointed out that a short piece of evidence that had been given by a friend of Mrs Gardiner, Martha Walker, corroborated Georgina's explanation about the labelled medicine bottle. In fact Wild told the court: 'I attach the very greatest importance to the evidence of Mrs Walker.'

So Wild should, because it had been one of the key parts of the evidence that had drawn Gardiner into the case and ultimately ended with his arrest, charge and trial for the murder. Finally, Wild turned to the question of blood. He contended that it was impossible for Gardiner to have committed the murder, not only without his wife knowing it, but also without getting blood on his clothing.

Dickens now summed up for the prosecution. He first cautioned the jury not to be misled by having any unreasonable sympathy for the Gardiner family. He said: 'There is hardly a crime which is committed which does not bring unhappiness, grief, sorrow and ruin upon the relatives of the guilty man.'

He pointed out that the defence had put great store in the piety of Gardiner and that it was in fact a series of facts that led to the belief that Gardiner was the murderer of Rose Harsent. First there were the buff envelopes, then the footprints and the inference that Rose was expecting his child.

On the night of the murder Dickens believed that there was incontrovertible evidence. First Gardiner was standing at his front door where he could see the light from Rose's bedroom. There was the evidence that the handwriting in the assignation letter was the same as Gardiner's hand. Then, of course, there was Morriss's testimony about the footprints.

The summing up by Mr Justice Lawrence began by focusing on the difference between direct evidence and circumstantial evidence. He asked the jury to consider the Doctor's Chapel incident in 1901:

> *Is that story a deliberate lie, for that is how it is met by the defence, or is it true? There is no halting ground between the two.*

He also turned to the testimony of John Guy and to the comments made by Rouse:

> *I think the accused must have been extremely unfortunate in the church to which he belongs. Do you believe Rouse, if you do not there is only one alternative; Rouse has committed wilful perjury for some reason or another.*

The judge also referred to the evidence given by the handwriting expert, Gurrin:

> *I am bound to say that Mr Gurrin is the best of his class; I have known two or three experts who did not give their evidence in the same modest way that Mr Gurrin did.*

He now looked at the question about the letter of assignation:

> *The question comes, and a very serious question, too, was that*

letter written by the accused or not? Upon whoever wrote that letter very strong suspicion is cast, because there is the letter making the midnight appointment; someone kept that appointment; and the result of that appointment was the death of the girl.

The judge seemed to discard the fact that Rose had committed suicide. He suggested that Gardiner's knife could have caused the injuries, but in itself the fact that Gardiner had cleaned the knife would mean nothing in other circumstances.

The jury finally retired at five o'clock. Two and a quarter hours later they returned. They indicated to the clerk that there was a problem. The clerk asked the jury foreman: 'Are you agreed upon your verdict?'

The foreman replied: 'No Sir.'

Mr Justice Lawrence turned to the foreman and said: 'You are not agreed? Is there any chance of you agreeing?'

The foreman replied again: 'No Sir.'

The judge pressed one last time: 'None whatsoever?'

The foreman replied: 'I'm afraid not.'

The judge then said: 'I mean if you are satisfied about that, it is my duty to discharge you. You have paid great attention to the case, and the only thing I can do is to make an order that you do not be called upon to serve on a jury again for seven years.'

In those times it was customary to place the accused man on trial for a third occasion, but for the prosecution to then offer no evidence. This would result in a full acquittal of the accused man. It would later transpire that eleven of the jurors believed Gardiner was not guilty.

Gardiner would, however, not have to face a third trial. It was initially believed that it would take place but the director of public prosecutions contacted Gardiner's solicitor, Mr Leighton, and said that he was not proposing a third trial.

Gardiner was released from Ipswich prison. He and his family left Peasenhall shortly afterwards. He shaved off his beard and was said to have opened a shop on the outskirts of London. There was rumour that on one occasion he visited Yoxford and that much later his children visited Peasenhall. There were various rumours about him; he was either working as a wheelwright or running a tobacconist shop or, indeed, that he had emigrated to North America.

One theory that seems to fit the majority of the evidence was that Rose was in fact the victim of an accident. An unknown man had written the letter of assignation and arranged to come and see Rose, but instead of finding her alive he found her dead at the foot of the stairs. The man was horrified and ran. Just before twelve, when her visitor was due to arrive, Rose came down the stairs. There was a newspaper under her arm, a lamp in one hand and a glass bottle in the other. Partway down the staircase she tripped and fell down the stairs and into the kitchen. The thud and scream was what Mrs Crisp heard. Had she gone to investigate, this is what she would have found. As Rose fell she may have stretched out her arm to prevent the lamp from breaking. This would explain why it was found in three pieces; the unbroken glass furthest away from the body, the reservoir of the lamp closest to her and then the holder. The paraffin escaped and ran along the floor and caught fire. The glass bottle in the other hand fell, smashed and cut her throat.

In fact there was a similar case when falling with a glass in his hand killed a boy. It cut him deeper than a razor would have.

So the theory goes that the wounds had to have been inflicted by glass rather than a knife, hence the jagged edges to the cuts. We do not know whether Rose Harsent's wounds were checked to see if there were any glass fragments. Rose probably pulled the glass out of her neck, flung it to the side and then fell into unconsciousness and died.

The former Scotland Yard detective sergeant, B. Leeson, put an alternative theory. He had left Scotland Yard after being wounded in the Battle of Sidney Street:

> *A sequel may be found in the evidence given at a murder trial some years ago. The victim had been done to death in her own house by someone who had visited her, and the evidence on which the prosecution relied to prove the case consisted of footprints which they endeavoured to move were made by the accused man. There was no doubt that the boots produced belonged to the prisoner, and fitted the prints, but he was acquitted for want of substantiating evidence. It is true that the footprints were made by someone passing to and from the prisoner's home, but to my mind the evidence, had it been weaved differently, would have proved the prisoner's wife to be the guilty person.*

Could it really be true that the frail, loyal wife of William Gardiner committed the killing? If so, what would have been the

Peasenhall cemetery, where Rose Harsent is buried.

motive, other than the certain knowledge that her husband was having an affair with Rose Harsent and that she was carrying his child? It would have been a simple task for her to borrow her husband's knife. Equally as easy to have donned the shoes and made that fateful crossing to Providence House and have committed murder on an unwitting Rose Harsent.

CHAPTER 4

Last Bus Ride to Death

The murder of Susan Long, 10 March 1970

Susan Margaret Long (18) had spent an enjoyable evening with her boyfriend at a dance hall on 10 March 1970. She caught the last bus, a No. 10, from Norwich bus station to Aylsham. It was just before 2230.

Susan had just bought her first car, but because her bus season ticket was still valid, she decided to make use of it for the last time. She arrived at Aylsham market place at 2300 and began the seven-minute walk to her home in Sir William's Lane. She never finished the walk.

Just before dawn a milkman's headlights picked up the shape of her body lying in a lane. She was less than a mile from home and she had been strangled.

There were clues for the police to follow up. There was a tiny speck of the murderer's blood. The attacker had a rare blood

Aylsham market place.

group; only one person in twenty-five had it. The second clue was a speck of paint, about the size of a pinhead. It belonged to a Ford saloon, made between 1959 and 1961. The car had later been re-sprayed maroon. Over the next twenty-five years the police managed to trace several re-sprayed Fords, but none of them could be linked to the murder. By now, of course, the car would have been long scrapped.

It was strongly believed that the murder had been carried out in a car and that Susan had probably been strangled with her own handbag strap. Speaking at the time of the murder, Detective Chief Inspector Reginald Taylor, said:

> *It appears someone gave her a lift and took her past her home to the spot where she was found. It is very unlikely Susan would have accepted a lift, especially so late at night, unless she knew the person extremely well.*

If the killer had thought that he was alone when he strangled and dumped Susan Long, he was mistaken. A woman had been there at the time, but failed to come forward until eighteen months after the murder. She wrote a letter to the police and explained:

> *I couldn't tell you then. I was still living with my husband, not now I'm separated I don't care.*

She claimed that she saw a man driving a car away at speed on the night:

> *That murder has preyed on my mind. He looked very frightened and in a terrible hurry. It was about 11.30 pm.*

There was a chance that the letter could be a hoax, perhaps with the motive of trying to frame someone for the murder. The police thought it could be genuine, but had no way of checking until they had a chance to talk to her. The letter writer never came forward, despite public appeals. As Reginald Lester (then head of Norfolk CID), said:

> *It was terribly sad, for Susan was an only child and such a lovely girl. Her murder came less than a year after the disappearance of April Fabb, but although there was much talk of the two cases being linked, there was no evidence to connect them.*

In early 1971, the police were investigating links between the Susan Long murder and three other similar murders in 1970. The murders took place in other parts of the country and the only real connection appeared to be the fact that the four girls had been hitchhiking. The police also believed that the killer had fled from the area as quickly as possible by using the motorway network.

The first of the connected murders had taken place on 14 March 1970. The victim, Jacqueline Ansell-Lamb (18), the daughter of an accountant, had been strangled with an electrical flex. Her body was found in woodlands at Mere, Cheshire. The second victim, also 18, was Rita Sawyer. Her partially clothed body was found in a cornfield near Harbury, Warwickshire, on 5 September. Rita had been stabbed to death. The final victim connected to Susan Long was Barbara May (24). She was a schoolteacher who had hitchhiked from London, up the M1. She had been strangled and her body was found at Ault Hucknall, near Chesterfield.

The police were clearly delighted with possibilities of the connections and the new leads that could emerge. Detective Chief Superintendent John Cass, confirmed that Cheshire police had visited Aylsham to trace a Cheshire man and his movements at the time that Susan was killed. The policeman in charge of the Jacqueline Ansell-Lamb enquiry added:

The crimes are so similar. The fact is that a man whose movements in Cheshire are being investigated was found to make trips to Norfolk at the time of the Aylsham murder.

It transpired that the police, after considerable investigations, came to the conclusion that despite the similarities and the Cheshire link, they could not connect the murders and no new information emerged from the cooperation between forces.

New and exciting evidence emerged in mid-1971. It was a letter contained in an envelope that appeared to be a wage packet. The envelope had a date on it and the number 8813. The number was presumed to be a cheque number and the amount was for £114. At the time it was believed to be either a money pay packet, or perhaps holiday pay. The name on the pay packet was Rogers.

By August 1971 the owner of the pay packet had been traced and eliminated. It was another cul-de-sac in the enquiry. During the enquiry itself the police had taken some 3,700 statements, a further 10,000 questionnaires had been completed and 835 blood samples tested. By any accounts, considering the period of the murder enquiry, the police effort had been massive.

At the time of the murder there was great fear in North Norfolk; it was only recently before that April Fabb had vanished. There was a distinctly uneasy feeling, despite the huge police hunts. Just two days before Christmas 1969, a man had tried to entice a young girl into his car on the Runton Road at Cromer. The man was never traced.

On the night of the murder, Molly and Derek Long could not get off to sleep until their daughter had arrived home. They patiently waited to hear her key in the front door lock. By midnight, they knew something must be wrong. Derek Long got up and got dressed and cycled to Aylsham to check to see if the last bus had arrived at its usual time. The bus had, so Molly Long called the police and asked them to trace the driver to find out whether Susan had been on the bus. He confirmed that he had seen her and that she had got off at Aylsham. Molly Long said:

> I simply can't tell you what it was like at that moment when we knew our Susan was missing. We feared the worst had happened, and stayed up all night worrying. When it started to get light, my husband and my brother started searching for Susan, but then the police said she had already been found. She was only about half a mile from home when they found her body. She was our only child; she meant the world to us.

Molly Long lost her husband to cancer in 1981 and often dreamed of Susan:

> In my dreams Susan is usually a little girl, full of smiles and laughter and Derek is often with her. I don't dream about her murder but I often think about it, wondering where and how her nightmare began on that awful night. The memories still hurt and they always will. It hurts when people talk of their children or grandchildren, when people are married, or when Susan's friends have children of their own. I hope whoever murdered Susan is tormented by what he did, and I simply want him to know I'm still here, I haven't forgotten. I'll always remember what he did to our beautiful daughter.

In all, the police had interviewed 20,000 people, including every adult and many of the children in Aylsham (population then 2,600). Police interviewed all of the male workers at Norwich

*RAF Coltishall where many of the servicemen were
questioned regarding the murder.*

Union, where Susan worked, all of the men based at RAF
Coltishall, including servicemen and others as far afield as
Singapore and the Gulf.

It had never been discovered what happened to Susan's
missing sling-back shoe and her blue and white, gold filigree
bracelet, which had also disappeared. Derek Long, in February
1971, had said:

*Susan's death is all I think about day and night. She was so
regular catching the last bus on a Tuesday night. Too regular.
It seems too much of a coincidence that the murder happened
the very last night she caught the bus. It was the last chance
the murderer had to get her on her own as she walked home in
the dark...and he took it.*

CHAPTER 5

The Headless Body of Cockley Cley

(Found 27 August 1974)

In the same month that the first grandfather, Russian cosmonaut, Flight Engineer Le Demin, went into space, the aptly named Andrew Head, a young farm worker, made a grisly discovery.

Andrew came across a woman's foot on the side of a path some 200 metres off the road near Cockley Cley. As he investigated he found the body of a headless woman lying in the tall weeds. The body was badly decomposed.

The body was dressed in a Marks and Spencer nightdress

Church at Cockley Cley.

and there was a large National Cash Register cover thrown over it. The ankles were tied to the thighs and the hands to the legs. A later post-mortem showed that the body had been pulled over a hard surface. The fingerprints did not match anything on file.

The police launched a massive enquiry. Some forty officers were assigned to the case. They interviewed 15,000 people, followed up 894 lines of enquiry, took 1,270 telephone calls, 700 statements and processed 6,750 questionnaires. They carried out intensive house-to-house enquiries over an area of twelve miles.

Despite the legwork, they struggled to even identify the victim. The 5 feet 2 inch woman had been dead for about two weeks. In the course of their enquiries they managed to trace 109 women who were believed to be missing.

The victim was white, about 23 years old, well-built and had not had any children. The nightdress was a standard Marks and Spencer product, of which around 10,000 had been sold. The 8 feet by 5 feet 6 inch light brown National Cash Registers sheet was more promising. It had NCR in gold letters printed on it and was one of only six made. Even the blood stains around the scene, on the nightdress and on the sheet revealed nothing in the way of clues.

Detective Superintendent Ivan Mead (Deputy Head of Norfolk CID) was put in charge of the investigation. At the heights of the investigations in 1974 he said:

> *The tying up seems to me to make it more easy to transport her. I don't think she was tied up and then killed. I am reasonably certain she was killed elsewhere and then taken to the spot, possibly in the boot of a car.*

Enquiries focussed on the sheet, made by a firm in Dundee, which had closed down in 1968. Despite extensive investigations, the police could not discover where the sheet had been or who had bought it.

The search now turned to two cars spotted near the scene on 9 August. The first was a British Leyland 1100 or 1300 cc car, dark coloured, with a female passenger. The woman 'appeared to be asleep', with her head laid against the passenger window. A second car, a green Mini Clubman, was also sought, having been seen near the area on several occasions.

Almost a year later, little hard evidence had been found, despite the huge number of leads that the police had followed.

Indeed, the police knew little more about the victim or the murderer than they had some forty-eight hours after the body was found.

Chief Inspector John Riches (Head of Dereham CID) said:

> *When it comes down to it, it is made awfully difficult by the fact here is a woman who has just dropped out of the environment she was in and no one bothered to report it. She obviously has no friends or family at all. This kind of enquiry opens your eyes to the fact that this kind of thing can happen – that there are people with no friends at all in the world.*

The prevailing theory was that she might have a connection with one of the British or American bases in the area, but extensive investigations showed that no one was missing.

In March 1977, three anonymous calls were made to Norfolk Police Headquarters. The caller, identifying himself only as 'Mr W', seemingly responded to a recent feature on television asked: 'Can you give me the day this happened?'

When asked to give his number so that a detective could call back, the man replied: 'I will ring back again in half an hour. I am Mr W. I have some information which may be of use.'

When Mr W called back, he was put through to Detective Chief Superintendent Reginald Lester, then Head of Norfolk CID. The first conversation took place at around 1140: 'Well, if she was alive on the Saturday at half past one, I seen a black American Negro do something very funny to a woman up the road – on the Saturday before you found her body. It was a black yank, a Negro. I seen him talking to a girl and I'm nearly certain he pushed her in the car.'

Lester asked if the caller knew the woman's name.

'No, no. I think she was a prossie. I'm not sure, 'cos there's a lot of prossies get up near there.'

Soon after the caller rang off and has not contacted the police since. The only other thing Mr W could add was that the woman was wearing a brown jersey with yellow squares or diamond patterns and that he thought there were two other men in the car.

By 1983, nine years had passed since the discovery. The case had not been closed. For a short while investigations were still underway when a headless body was found in Devon. Nick Mackley was one of three officers still following up leads and new information. He had received a letter about a hitchhiker in the area in 1974. The woman in question was traced to Maryland in America.

Ten years later, in 1993, the police were excited by a potential lead provided by Shirley Skinner, then living in Bradwell. The police believed they were on the verge of cracking the nineteen-year old mystery. Shirley was convinced that the victim was a friend of hers who had lived in Watton twenty-one years before. She said at the time:

> *The police should have taken me seriously 19 years ago. I could have told you then her surname and where she lived in Watton when the body was discovered, but a lot has happened in 19 years.*

Shirley had contacted the police, but they had not followed up her call. A woman, who Shirley had remembered as Maria, had lived above a chip shop in the High Street in Watton. Maria disappeared two years before the body was found.

The police launched an intensive four-week investigation into Shirley's claims. Police Constable Jonathan Jackson of Dereham police (one of the men who had been first at the murder scene in 1974), concluded:

> *We received several interesting phone calls and we were able to track her* [Maria] *back to 1969 when she worked at RAF Swanton Morley and from there to Watton, Reymerston and Australia!*

Maria was finally traced through relatives and friends, safe and sound and blissfully unaware of the furore back in Norfolk.

Had the head ever been found, police would have been able to identify the victim from her dental records. Police seemed to be convinced that the killer was a local, not someone who had brought the body to the spot to dump it. The track itself is difficult to find from the road and therefore someone with local knowledge is a distinct possibility. Approaching from the other direction, there would have been hundreds of acres of woodland to hide the body in.

Police believe the head was removed to ensure that not only was the body not identified by forensic means, but also that she may have been recognized as someone living and working in the area. It is possible the victim was tied up, assaulted and as a result was killed. The murderer or murderess then removed the head, wrapped up the body in the NCR sheet and headed off into the countryside in the early hours of the morning.

The killer or killers could not risk driving too far, so he or they chose the road to Cockley Cley, pulling off into a little known track. Probably, by the time the body would be found, the murderer would have left the area or even the country.

In all probability, the isolated spot meant that the body did not need to be buried; simply hiding it in the undergrowth would afford sufficient time before it was discovered.

In recent years there has even been speculation that it was a ritual killing. However, the mere fact that the police could not establish the identity of the victim meant that they could not even begin to pinpoint the area of the country associated with her. Occasionally new leads do come in and the police dutifully follow them up, always mindful of the efforts put into the case over the past thirty years or more.

Whether there was one killer or two, as some have suggested, the secret of the headless body remains with them. Perhaps the secret lies somewhere hidden in the police files?

The woodlands around Cockley Cley.

CHAPTER 6

Like a Dummy

The Gruesome Discovery on 26 August 1978

At about midday on Saturday, 26 August 1978 a timber merchant, Michael Watts, was walking in the woodland close to Dunston Hall. Watts lived on the Ipswich Road at Dunston, in a chalet just to the left of the lane that leads to Dunston Hall. At the time he owned the woods and they were under 100 metres from his own home. He had gone in there with an axe to cut down some trees.

Instead of finding suitable trees, he encountered a bundle of polythene. In fact Watts had seen the same bundle about three months beforehand, but had ignored it until this weekend. Something attracted him to it:

I walked into the wood and I just saw a bundle of polythene. I ignored it. I cut a tree down. Walking out I looked again. It looked a bit like a dummy or a guy you put on a bonfire. I ran my axe along the polythene, cut the polythene and realized it was a body.

View of Dunston Hall.

The body was, in fact, only about 10 metres from the lane leading to the hall. It was a closely wooded spot, full of larch trees. The wooded area is around 300 metres from the hall. Watts had lived there for around eleven years. He recollected seeing the bundle three months before:

> *I was clearing some trees on the land and I noticed it about six feet the other side of some barbed wire. I did not take any notice of it. I thought it was like a guy you would put on a bonfire. I thought it was a guy someone had thrown away.*

The only reason he'd had a really good look this time was that he was working on the other side of the barbed wire. When asked by reporters, he was sure that the body was clothed, but not completely sure.

When the police came it was found that the feet, still with their socks on, were sticking out of the bundle. Watts clearly had the impression that the body did not weigh very much because it rolled easily when he touched it. As soon as Watts realized what it was he immediately ran back home and telephoned the police.

The initial thoughts were that the body belonged to a man aged between 30 and 40 years. The police set up an incident room in the grounds of Vale Hospital in Swainsthorpe, which was just over a mile away from the scene.

The police confirmed that the body was very badly decomposed and that the man was between 5 feet 6 inches and 5 feet 8 inches tall. The body weighed around 9 stone 3lbs.

The Home Office Pathologist, David Harrison and the police surgeon, Dr James Hilton, examined the body in situ for around five hours. It was then removed from the wood and taken to Great Yarmouth General Hospital. Detective Chief Superintendent Reginald Lester, head of Norfolk CID, was put in charge of the case, supported by Detective Chief Inspector John Dye, the head of Dereham CID.

At the time the entertainer, Jimmy Lowne, owned Dunston Hall. He had owned the place for around two years and used it as a base for disabled musicians. Before that the twenty-one-bedroom hall had been used as a furniture store for forty years by the Norwich based business, Wallace King. Lowne, a member of the British Music Hall Society, was in the process of renovating the hall. He had bought it and five and a half acres of the surrounding land. Watts owned forty-five acres of the land at Dunston and he and his collie dog were often amongst the trees.

Two days later the results of the post mortem were released. They confirmed that the man had multiple stab wounds and that the cause of death was blood loss and shock.

The first task was for the police to compare what they knew about the body with descriptions of missing persons from the county and further a field. The man was found wearing a shirt, vest and denim trousers and he also had blue socks but no shoes.

Despite extensive enquiries and attempts to match missing persons' descriptions, Lester and his team drew a blank. Frustratingly for them this was the second mystery corpse to show up in Norfolk in the 1970s, the other one being the headless female of Cockley Cley.

As far as Jimmy Lowne, the owner of Dunston Hall was concerned, this was just another dreadful disaster related to the hall. He had had little but ill luck, despite his every effort to try and raise £50,000 to restore the hall. Neither he nor his visitors had ever seen the bundle; neither did they notice anything suspicious. Lowne said:

> *I regard this as the continuing saga of Dunston Hall. We had a fire last March, which destroyed a newly restored room and nearly £3,000 worth of musical equipment. I had a friend who was seriously injured in an accident on the road outside the hall and now I may have to give up the hall if I can't raise enough money to pay for it. I need about £20,000.*

CHAPTER 7

Man of Mystery

The Murder of Peter Miller, 9 December 1984

T he Reverend Richard Allington-Smith led the funeral service for a 24 year old man that had been found by his brother in the kitchen of a property in Camden Place, Great Yarmouth. The body had been found on Sunday, 9 December 1984, but the funeral had not taken place until May 1985. The extraordinarily long period between the murder and the funeral gives something of a clue as to the problems that the police had in trying to piece together the jigsaw of the murder victim, Peter Miller's life.

Back in December 1984 the Great Yarmouth police believed that they had some positive leads. They had scoured the area around the small terraced house, where Peter Miller's body had been found. He had been lodging with his brother, Anthony and his wife.

The couple had left Peter at home at midday to visit some of their relatives. It was the opinion that Peter had died within three hours of his body being discovered at 1945 on that Sunday evening. Detective Superintendent Bunn said:

We believe he was stabbed with a knife. But death was certainly not instantaneous. There was very little sign at all of a fight, although there were some signs of a struggle.

At the time the police were encouraged by the information they were receiving from local residents. But all too soon the trail would go cold.

Miller's brother Anthony revealed to the coroner in June 1985 that Peter had been in a mood the morning of his death. They had left him watching football on television:

When I arrived home I found the door was open. I saw Peter lying on the floor. I didn't realize it was Peter at first because it was dark and there weren't any lights on in the house. I just saw a dark form. I went straight through to the kitchen to turn a light on and saw it was Peter lying face down in a pool of blood. I turned him over and tried to wake him up but there was no sign of life.

Anthony had found his brother wearing a tracksuit bottom and just one shoe. The jumper that he had been wearing earlier was on the floor beside him:

I laid his jumper under his head. I then noticed something in the air which was making me cough and burned my eyes. At first I thought it was gas and tried to pull Peter out of the room. I didn't think he was dead and that's why I was concerned about the gas.

Anthony said there was no sign of a struggle but there were bloodstains. The letter rack on the back of the door had been broken and there was a small CS gas spray canister lying on the floor near the door.

Dr David Harrison, who had carried out the post mortem, confirmed that the only injury was a single stab wound in the upper left chest. It was about 17 centimetres deep. It was Harrison's belief that Peter Miller had died at some point between 1700 and 1900. He would have been conscious for the first fifteen minutes and might possibly have been an hour after his attack.

The police confirmed that there was a trail of blood from the front door. There were traces of hair, which were believed to have come from a wig.

Shortly after the killing Peter Miller's elder sister, Linda Kevern, had told the police that her brother had become withdrawn in the months that led up to his death. She believed that he feared his life was in danger:

It's gone through my mind that someone was looking for him. Myself, I think someone went round there to frighten Peter, and went too far.

She said that there had been a change in his character in July 1984. He admitted he had been in trouble with the police, but the police remained baffled as to who would want to murder or scare the unemployed man.

Peter Miller was one of eight children and his mother, Sylvia Miller, made the almost unprecedented move of calling her own press conference just eight days into the hunt for the killer. She told the press that she was prepared to meet anyone hiding the person. She was positive that someone was protecting the killer:

> *I must meet this person on my own. I want them to contact me at any time, day or night, and I shall meet them wherever they say. There will be no police, I must meet this person on my own.*

Detective Superintendent Bunn could not confirm or deny that the police were looking for anyone who may have threatened Peter Miller:

> *It's a possibility we can't rule out, but we have got nothing to corroborate it at the moment. We have sightings of him all round the town, with girls and friends, so he certainly didn't give the impression of being in fear. But that doesn't mean it didn't exist beneath the surface.*

The police also admitted that their suspicions did seem to centre around a mystery man that had been directed to the house in Camden Place shortly before the body was discovered by Anthony Miller. Despite numerous interviews no one could tell the police anything about the man who was described as being in his mid-twenties, around 5 feet 6 inches, with light blonde, shoulder-length hair. He was also believed to have been of slim build, wearing casual clothes, with an earring in his left ear and a tattoo on his right forearm.

Linda Kevern had said: 'This town is not big enough for people not to know what has gone on.'

Certainly the killer must have had blood on him or her and the family were convinced that someone was shielding the killer.

There was more on the mystery man. It was compiled in a police diary, which proved that on at least four occasions the blonde man, who was also described as wearing glasses, was seen with Peter Miller. The first sighting was on Wednesday, 5 December. Peter Miller and the man were seen at 1200 on Blackfriar's Road. They were walking towards Camden Road. The man was described as wearing a grey or green zip-up bomber jacket. Three hours later the pair were seen on King Street, outside the St George's Arts Centre.

Two days later, on Friday, 7 December, the two men were

Great Yarmouth town wall on Blackfriars Road.

seen in the Blackfriar Tavern having a drink at 1930. This time the mystery man was wearing a pair of jeans and a jumper.

On Sunday 9th, at 1200, the day of the murder, they were again seen on Blackfriar's Road, near the archway of the town wall. The man was wearing the same zip-up bomber jacket and a pair of dark trousers. He was seen again later that day at 1905 and again at 2130, this time on West Street.

The police were desperate for this man to come forward, as Inspector McDonnell said:

> *We hope this man will come forward – if only to be eliminated from the inquiries and save us wasting any more time on this line. Or, if he doesn't come forward, we hope this will jog someone's memory, who might be able to come forward and give us any further descriptions of him.*

The man did not come forward and neither could any witnesses positively identify him. This was still the state of affairs when

Peter Miller was buried in May 1985. The police admitted in the June that they were still baffled, as Detective Inspector Alan Whittaker admitted: 'It's a murder that's totally baffling the police in Yarmouth. A local boy with local connections and we just can't get near it.'

It seemed certain to the police that Peter Miller knew his killer. There was the bizarre, unexplained presence of hair from a wig and also the illegal self-defence CS gas spray canister. The police could not be sure whether the CS gas belonged to Miller or whether it was used as part of the attack. It was clear that the murderer had not broken into the house, but had been let in. The police thought they had a useful lead in tracking down the source of the CS gas, but this, like all of the other leads, led nowhere.

Despite rewards being offered and an intensive hunt involving seventy detectives from all across Norfolk, no one was arrested, no one charged and all of the vital questions remained unanswered. The police never traced the murder weapon. They were certain, however, that the murderer was not a local, but must have been staying in Great Yarmouth since the summer of 1984 at least.

In all the case involved 100 police officers, over 1,000 statements were taken and 2,500 inquiries followed up. At one point the Miller family even offered the house where he was murdered as a reward to catch the killer. As Anthony Miller said: 'We've offered the house because we don't want to move back into the house for obvious reasons – and because we want the person to be caught.'

Despite being worth £12,000 at the time, this neither brought the family nor the police closer to the killer.

CHAPTER 8

Murdered in France

The Murder of Lorraine Glasby and Paul Bellion, August 1986

Lorraine Glasby was 28 years old and she taught craft, design and technology at Diss High School in Norfolk. Her partner, Paul Bellion, had similar teaching expertise and was working at the Rosemary Musker High School in Thetford.

It was the summer holiday of 1986 and the couple, recently engaged to be married, had just moved into their idyllic new home, Laundry Cottage, in Garboldisham near Diss. The day after, they left for their summer holiday cycling in northern France. Over the next few weeks they would be seen riding around the French countryside by several witnesses and, indeed, they would even be spotted apparently waiting for a ferry back across the English Channel.

For some unknown reason, one or more kidnappers snatched them and bundled them into the back of an orange Volkswagen van. The vehicle had previously been stolen from Germany. The police

Garboldisham Church.

Diss town sign.

The mere at Diss.

would later connect the couple with the vehicle when they found some of Lorraine's hair in it.

As the French prosecutor in Dinan, Eric Bouillard, who led the enquiry, admitted in August 2005, nineteen years after the brutal execution of the young couple:

> *We have found in the whole of France eleven cases that have come up with the same way of killing. We have a central service for DNA, which is a new one, and we have to be prudent and to compare any DNA to be sure that it is a sole killer.*

Paul was a fluent French speaker. He had lived in Norfolk for five years. Both he and Lorraine loved France, the country's people and its culture. No one would believe it when the couple failed to return to their schools in September for the start of the new term. It was only then that the alarm was raised. As it was their bodies were not discovered until 1 October 1986. They had both been shot at close range.

From what the French police could ascertain, the couple had been bundled into the orange Volkswagen van and driven away. For some reason they had been first made to kneel then tied back-to-back. They were then gagged. There was evidence that Lorraine had tried to make an escape at some point as she had a bullet wound on her leg. Nonetheless the pair had been executed at very close range with a shotgun. Their bodies were left in a shallow grave in a cornfield at Dinan in Brittany.

At the time the French police failed to track down any potential suspects after a hunter had found the bodies in the field. The police dragged ponds and rivers, but failed in their attempts to find the couples' bicycles or property. The French police had a lot of theories but no real evidence. At first they believed that it was a military style execution and then they placed the blame on terrorists.

There was certainly DNA evidence at the scene, but even up to this point the French have failed to link it with any known criminal or individual serving time in France in one of their prisons.

Nineteen years after the murders a prisoner in a French jail was said to have confessed to a cellmate that he was responsible for the double killing. The individual, unnamed, had been jailed for arts thefts. Immediately the prosecutor, Bouillard, brought both of the prisoners to Paris, where they were interviewed at length. The alleged murderer denied that he had said this to his cellmate, but the French were now determined to re-investigate the case and review the evidence. This constituted the first new line of enquiry for many years.

Bouillard told the British press in June 2005:

Four years ago a prisoner said to his friend that he had killed two persons in western France. He did not say anything else. There have been two double murders in that area – one in 1979 of two Belgians and the English couple in 1986 – it is really strange because the prisoner is the son of the person who was suspected of murdering the two Belgians, and we don't know exactly why this has happened.

There was, however, considerable doubt about the trustworthiness of the cellmate. He had lied to the police in the past, hoping to receive some kind of reward or better treatment. Bouillard explained:

> *He had received lots of other confidences from prisoners, and the information he gave in one important case was wrong, so we are being prudent.*

By August 2005 Bouillard confirmed that the French authorities were looking at other murders in France over the past twenty years. They were focussing on cases where victims had been murdered with a shotgun at close range. Bouillard confirmed that the investigations would take two or three months to complete. He promised to ensure that the families of the two British victims would be the first to be informed if something were discovered.

The brutal murder of Lorraine and Paul had had an understandably marked effect upon their families. For many years the families had heard nothing from the French authorities and it was their opinion that the French, after an initial flurry of activity, had simply lost interest in the case. There had been some fresh hope in early 2002, when a letter from the Foreign and Commonwealth Office had informed the families that the case was being reopened. Ultimately, there was no new news, there were no new breakthroughs and the theories, such as they were, came to nothing.

In October 2006 Eric Bouillard confirmed that he was likely to finally close the case. This was despite the pleas of both British and French police to step up the investigations. There had been similarities between the executions of two Belgians in 1979, but beyond that little had been proved.

Almost twenty years to the day the hunter, Louis Trehel, now 83 years old, accompanied British journalists to the very field where he had made the grisly discovery. He had found the bodies hidden under 6 feet high maize stalks. The couple were naked from the waist up, tied back-to-back and gagged. The farmer who owned the land said:

> *There's more fallow land now than there was at the time and there aren't any rabbits any more, just pheasants. The man who found the bodies was out hunting with his dogs. The British couple were shot in the back of the neck. It was a professional job; not someone from around here.*

It is, however, widely believed by French locals that they were in fact killed with a hunting rifle, a commonplace weapon in the area. The locals also point out that only someone with a local knowledge would have found such a remote place to execute the couple, as it took more than a month for their bodies to be found.

It also transpired that the French had somehow lost the DNA sample from the stolen Volkswagen van. Bouillard had also closed the case without telling anyone in 1991. Under French law, after ten years, cases are deleted and prosecutions can never be brought. It had been Tony Blair in 1999 that had argued for the case to be reopened. The French prisoner had made his partial confession in 2001. It was at that point that the case was finally reopened.

The investigating officer was a police captain from St Malo, Pascal Huche, the link with St Malo being that this was the last known place where the couple had been seen alive and well. Huche's theory was that the French prisoner had murdered the British couple as a copycat execution, in an attempt to clear his father's name, as he was the prime suspect in the murder of the Belgian couple.

The French Interior Ministry banned Huche from talking to the media without express permission and ultimately the police captain was moved to the French CID in Paris, leaving no one to actively investigate the case.

Bouillard said of Huche's theory:

> *There is no evidence to support his theory, which is purely intellectual. He believes that man's father killed the Belgians and he copied the killing in 1986. The scenario is far-fetched and not supported by evidence.*

Of the lost DNA sample, which could have linked the murderer(s) to the van and the abduction of the British couple, Bouillard said:

> *Tens of thousands of Euros have been spent on DNA tests. Dozens of men have been deployed. It's true that one DNA sample went missing after a lab closed, but it was not a crucial one. If the case is closed it will be because there's not enough evidence around.*

This is scant reassurance for the families of the murdered Norfolk couple. The constant waiting for news has drained them. Elizabeth Bellion, Paul's mother, said in 2005:

> *Something like this can either bring you closer or tear you apart. My comfort is having a picture of Paul here and talking to him in the morning and nighttimes. They say time is a healer. No it isn't but you adapt.*

CHAPTER 9

Happy Go Lucky

The Murder of Andrew Pilch 9 September 1990

On 13 September 1990, an unnamed woman and two men were helping police with their enquiries regarding the murder of 34 year old, Andrew Pilch, an unemployed computer operator. He lived in the idyllic Rosemary Cottage, Church Street, Elsing near Dereham. His 27 year old wife, Sarah, found his body. The couple had two children, Louis (5) and Eleanor (4).

Sarah and Andrew seemed very happy together, but it was not all as it appeared. By the following day, the police confirmed that one of the three people they had arrested was Sarah. A fourth person, another man, had also been arrested. On 16 September, the three men appeared in a special police court at Thetford Police Station. They were named as Andrew Charles Watts (21) an unemployed man of no fixed abode, Kevin Michael Hearle (23) and his brother Nigel Peter Hearle (25) both from Easton. They were granted legal aid and none of them applied for bail.

The inquest took place on 20 September. The Dereham Coroner, Chris Starling, stated that a post mortem had taken place and it revealed that Andrew had been asphyxiated. He was either strangled or had had a blow or blows to the neck.

At the committal hearing, the three men denied murdering Andrew Pilch and the date was finally set for the trial in June 1991. The trial opened with the prosecution claiming that Kevin Hearle had been behind the plot to murder Andrew. He was Sarah's lover and she had recently dumped him. Hearle had lived as a lodger in the Pilch house and had been tormented by Sarah making love to her husband after the affair was over.

Graham Parkins, QC, prosecuting, claimed: 'Kevin wanted to get Mr Pilch out of the way because of a mixture of sexual jealousy and financial gain.'

It had been originally thought that Andrew had died of either

Elsing Village sign.

a heart attack or a cerebral haemorrhage, but a pathologist found strangle marks around his neck that proved that he had been murdered.

Kevin Hearle had brought his brother and Andrew Watts into the conspiracy to kill, argued the prosecution, to help him kill the victim and then to provide an alibi. Sarah Pilch, on the other hand claimed that she had seen all three of the men at her house that day, despite them claiming that they were in Hemsby.

Sarah had begun her affair with Hearle soon after he had moved into the house. Their sexual relationship started when they had come back from a nightclub during a period when her husband was away with the Territorial Army. Sarah admitted that she had had other sexual relationships outside the marriage, Hearle had become very jealous of this and wanted her to stop. Sarah also accused her husband of violence towards her and said that divorce had been discussed. She absolutely denied anything to do with the murder of her husband.

Under cross-examination, she was accused of lying about how she had found her husband, and her various sexual relationships. Ernle Money, representing Nigel Hearle said: 'By misleading the police you were creating a sufficient smoke screen to protect yourself. Why did you not help the police bring your husband's killers to justice?'

She replied: 'I do not know why I did not say anything. I should have told them straight away. I will regret for the rest of my life that I did not tell them straight away.'

Parkins then told the jury that Sarah was to gain £100,000 from a life insurance policy on the death of her husband.

Home Office pathologist Dr David Harrison told the court that in his opinion more than one person carried out the murder. Given Andrew Pilch's size and strength, despite the fact that he had cerebral palsy, he would have needed to be held down to be strangled.

As the trial drew to a close, there was sudden chaos. The court was told that a witness statement was missing and the trial was immediately halted. Mr Justice Hognall discharged the jury after ruling that the three men could not be fairly tried. He ordered that the case be restarted.

It recommenced on 8 July 1991 and familiar ground was covered. The new jury heard transcripts of Kevin Hearle's police interviews. He only admitted his sexual relationship with Sarah in the third interview, saying that he loved her and that their affair had lasted just two months. He admitted having been told by Sarah that her husband hit her, he was also accused of following Sarah around 'like a little puppy'.

A fellow remand prisoner, Paul Briley appeared next. It had been one of his statements that had gone adrift and had caused the termination of the first trial. He explained to the court that he had met the defendants in prison. Kevin Hearle told him that he had been having an affair with the murder victim's wife:

They told me the husband had found out and they were going to sort it out. All three of them had travelled to Elsing in Nigel's car. We were joking about it in the prison's exercise yard and I made the comment about Watts being the murderer. He lost his temper and said 'I suppose you think it was me that killed him with the sash cord'. They kept saying they didn't do it and they would get off. And they kept changing their stories all the time.

George Carter-Stephenson, representing Andrew Watts said that Briley was a: 'Thoroughly dishonest person who was prepared to say whatever was necessary to manipulate situations to his advantage.'

The court had heard that Briley had a string of convictions for burglary and theft and was awaiting trial for three similar offences. Hearle would later deny that he said anything of the sort.

Kevin Hearle now appeared. He claimed that he had only heard of the death of Andrew Pilch the day after it had happened:

I felt absolutely shocked. I felt sorry for the children and for Sarah. I felt a little gleeful. I felt sorry for the family, but happy I could be with Sarah.

Parkins, prosecuting, accused him of having got rid of Sarah's husband so that he could start a new life with his widow:

You did not see your relationship with Sarah as simply a sexual affair. You wanted it all. You wanted the ready-made family that you liked a lot and the woman you cared a great deal for.

Hearle denied this accusation. He refuted the claim that the affair was over, in fact he confirmed that it had carried on up to the point of Andrew's death: 'We made love loads of times in the house, in the car, down at her parent's house and in nearly every room in her home.'

Doctor Vesha Djurovic, a forensic expert claimed that the marks around the neck confirmed that one person could have strangled Andrew with a cord, even a well-built woman.

Mr Justice Ognall in his summing up damned Sarah Pilch as a 'proven liar'. He went on to say:

Elsing Church, near Dereham.

Whatever Andrew Pilch's alleged failings, and we only have her word for it, she had repeatedly betrayed him as a wife, most recently with Kevin Hearle. You can find that a witness is wholly feckless and utterly immoral, you can find that a witness is a proven liar, Sarah Pilch obviously is.

Although not on trial herself, it seemed that many in the court believed that Sarah knew an awful lot more about the death of her husband than she was prepared to say. Helena Kennedy QC, acting for Kevin Hearle said Sarah was a physically fit size 16 and that her deep contempt for her husband was the motive.

Family and friends of the three men wept with joy when they were acquitted after serving ten months on remand.

Year's later, wealthy businessman Peter Pilch, Andrew's father, was still desperately trying to track down his son's murderer. By 1995, he had spent £400,000 on private investigations.

In the early days when the police were questioning Sarah Pilch, they certainly considered her to be the prime suspect. It was only in the last of her four statements that she made any mention of seeing the three men at the scene of the murder. The judge believed that she had lied, either to shield her lover or to make sure that she collected the £100,000. Sarah Pilch never collected the money as the insurance company could prove that the payments had lapsed.

Sarah Pilch had claimed that she and her husband were 'sexually incompatible'. The judge had ruefully replied:

You may conclude that, bearing in mind her sexual appetites, in view of her liaisons, it may be difficult to find anyone she was sexually compatible with.

As it transpired, the only direct evidence against any of the three men was that provided by Sarah Pilch. We can only surmise why she did not tell the police earlier and why she laid a false trail.

CHAPTER 10

Black Christmas

The Murder of Brian Andrews,
10 September 1990

Forty-six year old Brian Andrews, a former Coldstream Guardsman and father of six, lost his fight for life on 10 September 1990. He had severe injuries to the face, head, neck and stomach. The 6 feet 6 inch, 22 stone Andrews probably died as a result of a single punch, which had knocked him to the pavement in a ferocious street brawl. It was apparent that he had received numerous kicks after he had hit the floor.

Andrews had been out drinking in Norwich with two of his sons, Robert and Richard. It was a family ritual to visit the Festival House pub each weekend.

Three men would find themselves charged with the murder. Two were Royal Marine Commando lance corporals, Darren

Princes Street. The pub where the murder victim was drinking can be seen at the end of the street.

Robson, then 22 and Peter Baldwin, then 23. Both men were stationed at the Royal Marine Base, Arbroath. The third man was Allan Robson, then 22, Darren's brother.

According to a witness, Donna Scotter, it was Andrews that had encouraged one of his sons to start the brawl. The Robson brothers and Baldwin had got into an argument with Robert Andrews outside the pub. Robert was ready for a fight and when the Robson brothers and Baldwin walked off towards Princes' Street he kicked one of them from behind. Robert Andrews was told to 'leave it out', but according to Donna Scotter a fight was inevitable when Brian Andrews, together with two friends, Andrew Yull and Alistair Mooney, arrived in support. They had all been drinking heavily. As Scotter would later tell the court: 'You could see it was going to be a big, furious fight. Their eyes showed they were angry.'

Brian Andrews appeared to have thrown the first punch and then encouraged Robert to attack them. The Robson brothers and Baldwin quickly gained control and were kicking and punching their opponents on the ground. Scotter claimed to hear Brian Andrews's head crack on the pavement. She screamed 'you're going to kill him. You're going to kill him'. She then claimed that one of the three men continued his attack and stamped on Brian Andrews's throat.

Brian Andrews was rushed to Addenbrooke's Hospital, but died on the following Monday.

The family had been prepared for the worst, having been told just how serious his injuries were. His wife, Carol, had stayed by his bedside throughout.

Shortly after Brian's death his sister, Jean Turner, said:

> *We want justice done. They have not only taken the life of a man of forty-six, they have ruined the lives of his children and his wife. We are angry and bitter. If I could get my hands on the people who did this I would go to town on them like they went to town on my brother.*

The police quickly identified the three men in question. In fact the police had arrested a total of seven people in connection with the incident; four had been arrested shortly after the fight and three more the following day. Four men had since been released. The police confirmed that two of the men still in custody were from Norwich and one was from the Midlands. Just a week later the Robsons and Baldwin appeared at a four-minute hearing at Norwich Magistrate's Court. They were charged with the murder of Brian Andrews and remanded in custody.

Over a year later the three men found themselves before Mr Justice Boreham at Norwich Crown Court. They all denied murder and had pleaded not guilty to violent disorder. The court heard that Baldwin alone had been interviewed fourteen times. During the two days of questioning he denied attacking Andrews. During his twelfth interview Baldwin finally changed his story and admitted kicking the former guardsman.

It had been Baldwin's first visit to Norwich. They had been drinking in the city and had been confronted by Robert Andrews. He had hurled verbal abuse at them and then followed them. Baldwin claimed that Brian Andrews was one of ten people who trailed them along Prince's Street and that he had tried to calm the situation down, but that Andrews and the aggressive group with him started a fight. Baldwin claimed he had acted in self-defence, but admitted that he had kicked one of the men five times, as well as hitting Brian Andrews. Baldwin 'went mad' and 'blew his top'. This was after Baldwin's neck chain was broken and his shirt was torn.

In admitting to affray Baldwin was jailed for twenty-one months, but there still remained the thorny problem of the

The narrow part of Princes Street before it connects with Tombland.

The junction of Tombland and Princes Street.

murder accusation. After six days in court Mr Justice Boreham told the jurors that he would be directing them to find the three men not guilty of murder. The principle problem lay with the expert medical witness, Dr David Harrison. It was his opinion that Brian Andrews had died from head injuries caused by a severe beating. However, under cross-examination he had conceded that Brian Andrews could have died as a result of the first punch, or as he hit the ground.

The court had already heard that the first punch aimed at Brian Andrews had been thrown by Darren Robson. It was accepted that this first punch had been thrown in self-defence. As a consequence, the murder charges could not safely remain. The judge said:

The prosecution have never suggested that they could ask you to find that the first blow was unlawful. It is accepted that the blow was struck in reasonable self-defence.

There were legal arguments, but the fact remained that the source of Brian Andrews's injuries could not be accurately assigned. After nine days the Robson brothers walked free, having been found not guilty of murder, violent disorder and affray.

On the court steps Darren Robson said:

My condolences go out to the man's family but justice has been done. It's been a very traumatic 15 months for me and the family but I am now anxious to get back to the Royal Marines and my career.

The Robson family had sat nervously waiting for the jury to consider the final two charges of violent disorder and affray. They were delighted when their sons were found not guilty. Their father, Bert, had never doubted their innocence. He said the whole family would enjoy a wonderful Christmas.

This would not be the Christmas looked forward to by the Andrews family. As Gertrude Andrews, Brian's mother said:

I was disgusted with the sentence. My son is dead. He has been put down as a villain and he wasn't. He used to love kids; he had six of his own and was always mucking about and playing. And he would pack old ladies' bags for them in a supermarket. Last Christmas was black and it is going to be black this Christmas.

It had indeed been a black Christmas for Gertrude Andrews. Christmas 1990 had seen her coming to terms with the death of her son, nicknamed 'Big'un'. She had spent 1991 waiting for the trial and then on the Monday before the trial was due to begin her 72 year old husband had died.

Brian Andrews's widow felt very bitter about the conclusion of the trial: 'My six kids have been left without a dad.'

The only one to pay in her view had been Baldwin, jailed for just twenty-one months:

It's not much for a life. I'm just angry, but there's nothing anyone can do now. He was a good dad, but his six kids haven't got one now. He was the life and soul of the party. Our house now seems so empty and cold. You get up each day and do what you've got to do.

In a later twist for the Andrews family, Richard Andrews was sentenced to two years for setting fire to a community hut, burglary, attempted theft and handling stolen goods in 1994. His defence barrister, Michael Clare, said of the unemployed Richard that he was struggling to cope, having seen his father murdered when he was just 17 years old. Richard Andrews was severely depressed, self-mutilated himself and always sought

Looking up Princes Street from Tombland.

attention. He was a repeat offender, but always admitted to his crimes when the police interviewed him.

In a mad, drink-fuelled few minutes in September 1990 the Andrews family had suffered yet another tragedy, which would resonate for years after Brian Andrews's death, severely affecting at least one of his sons.

Peter Baldwin's promising military career was over. We can only guess the lasting impression that that night had on the Robson brothers and their family.

It had been, as the prosecuting council, Graham Parkins, had said, a 'quite brutal and unnecessary attack'. He had gone on to say: 'The Marines were good soldiers and highly trained professional fighting men. They were more than a match for the opposing side.'

At the time Darren Robson was known to be an accomplished boxer, but it will never be known precisely which blow would finally end Brian Andrews's life.

CHAPTER 11

Branded a Murderer

The Killing of Sharon Tyler, 12 November 1991

Mechanic, Ivan Smith, of Tilney All Saints, near King's Lynn, walked away a free man on 7 July 1995. It was the end of a nightmare that had begun on 12 November 1991.

Unwittingly, Smith, a neighbour of Sharon Tyler, mother of two, had entered her home after hearing shouting. He found Sharon, savagely stabbed, lying on the kitchen floor.

Detective Chief Superintendent Alan Smith headed the investigation. There was no sign of forced entry and urgent enquiries began. Smith was interviewed, as was Michael Bunn, who lived in the same house as Sharon and was her boyfriend at that time.

By late November, police were still hunting for the elusive breakthrough in the case; cars were stopped as they passed through the village and house-to-house enquiries continued. Police hunted the drivers of a Ford Fiesta and a Transit van. Two men and a woman had been arrested, but later released without charge. There was still no sign of the murder weapon. The police were convinced that Sharon knew the murderer.

In December, just as the inquest into the murder was being held, the police arrested Ivan Smith for the killing. Smith denied the charges and was remanded to appear before King's Lynn magistrates on 2 January 1992.

As it transpired, Fakenham Magistrates committed Smith to trial in May 1992; the case would not go to court in Norwich until 1993. The evidence linking Smith to the murder scene appeared damning.

Smith was accused of having entered Sharon's home in the evening of 12 November 1991. Sharon's children were asleep upstairs and Michael Bunn was out playing darts at the pub. Crucially, it was alleged that Smith had a twenty-eight-minute window to carry out the crime while his wife and a friend went to collect a Chinese takeaway.

Police had found a knife with bloodstains in Smith's house, used, they argued, to inflict the thirteen stab wounds. A set of Sharon's door keys was also found in his cesspit. Sharon's blood had been found on Smith's trousers and jumper (Sharon's blood group was rare and only 8 per cent of the population had this type). A piece of twine, which had been found under Sharon's body, matched twine found in Smith's garden. He seemed doomed and, for the time being, he was. It would be forensic evidence that would condemn him, but later be his salvation.

Smith bitterly denied the accusations, sticking to his original statement that he had responded to hearing shouting and an argument emanating from Sharon's house.

David Stokes QC, prosecuting, told the court on 9 June that there were in fact ten wounds; some so severe they had caused extensive internal damage. One stab wound had severed Sharon's spinal cord; she would have been instantly paralysed. After recounting the knife evidence, the presence of the twine and the bloodstains on Smith's clothes, Stokes conjured the scene moments before the killing.

Stokes pictured Sharon making coffee for the killer; as she turned, he said, Smith had struck. This explained the presence of blood and coffee on Smith's shoes. However, the only footprints in the kitchen were that of Michael Bunn, Sharon's boyfriend.

Valerie Crowden was called to the witness box. She had been with Smith and his wife on the night of the murder. She stated that she and Susan Smith had left Ivan with his two children at 2010 to collect a Chinese takeaway. They returned in under half-an-hour and found Smith and the two children next door in Sharon Tyler's home. Smith told her that Sharon had been attacked and he had called an ambulance. Crowden could not remember exactly what had happened that night, clearly the episode had shocked her; she had broken down, sobbing, while giving her evidence.

John Westwood, ambulance technician, attended the scene. He gave evidence that he had found Sharon lying face down in about a litre of blood. She had been cold; her eyes fixed and there had been no pulse.

Michael Bunn gave evidence, admitting that he was a convicted burglar, but that he was playing darts at the time of the murder. He told the court that Sharon had had an affair with

Keith Simper when he was in prison and she had also had a relationship with another man Bunn had known in prison. Despite
this, Bunn and Sharon had been together for seven years.

The prosecution then turned to the keys found in Smith's
cesspit. It was alleged that Sharon's front door key was missing
before Bunn went out that night. The key, found in Smith's
cesspit was the missing key and the cesspit had not been
emptied for five years.

Paul Smith was called to the witness box. He had lived with
Susan Smith in the past. Paul Smith was a former butcher and
when he had split up with Susan she had kept one or two of his
knives.

A forensic scientist, Stephen Brown, was called to the stand
on 11 June. Crucially, he had found bloodstains matching
Susan's on Smith's clothing and shoes. These were only tiny
droplets and he agreed that they could have got there by moving
the body.

Smith appeared in the witness box on 14 June and recounted
the same story of finding Sharon's body. The prosecution had
alleged that he had changed his story when he told them he had
seen the body through the kitchen window. Smith denied that he
was having an affair with Sharon and, to the contrary, did not
find her attractive. He denied knowledge of the key in the
cesspit and explained that the blood on his jumper and shoes
probably got there when he found Sharon. He was at a loss to
explain the blood's presence on his trousers as he was wearing
a boiler suit.

Consultant pathologist, Dr David Harrison, testified that the
attack was made from behind and that the probable cause of
death was shock and blood loss.

The jury returned on 16 June 1993 and on the following day,
with a 10-1 majority (one jury member had been discharged due
to ill health), they found Smith guilty. They had taken four and a
half hours to reach their verdict. Smith was sentenced to life.

On 5 December 1995, Smith took his case to the Appeal
Court in London. The police had still failed to suggest a motive
for the attack, but the diluted bloodstains on Smith's clothes still
appeared damning. In the retrial at the Old Bailey the court
heard that Sharon had had sex with someone, other than
Michael Bunn, just hours before her death. There had been a
'mix-up' over scientific slides, which had led to the 'mistaken
conclusion' that bodily fluids proving this were not present. The
inevitable logic was that the murderer and Sharon's last partner

were the same person.

Dr Brown had not carried out DNA tests that would have excluded Smith. Smith had supplied a sample of his DNA; it had not been crosschecked with samples found at the scene.

Smith was cleared on 7 July 1995. The judge, Henry Pownall, described the forensic work on the case as being 'disgraceful and unprofessional'. He went on to say that the scientific evidence was 'shot through with unreliable conclusions'. Pownall concluded:

> *To describe this as exceptional and unusual is charitable in the extreme. Certainly it was so extraordinary it is very important to consider its effect on the evidence as a whole.*

Sharon's mother said: 'Whoever killed her is free, and for two years we thought the murderer was in prison.'

Smith's solicitor, Stephen McGregor commented: 'He [Smith] had lost a good job as an engineering fitter. His wife has left him as have his two children.'

Smith's mother, Doris, had collapsed when her son was cleared of the charges. Smith had spent eighteen months of his life sentence in prison. He had always strongly protested his innocence. He returned home and considered taking legal action against the Norfolk Constabulary.

The case remains unsolved. It is certainly the case that Sharon knew her killer; whether she had had sex with him that day is not known, nor whether this had been the cause of the murder. It is plausible that someone sought to frame Smith for the killing, knowing he might have access to the house and planting evidence to link him to the murder scene.

There had been sufficient evidence to suggest Smith's guilt, but even the most rudimentary forensic tests would have proved conclusively whether he had a case to answer. Had these forensic tests been made at the time, then the police efforts could have been redirected at finding the true culprit. Many avenues of investigation had been abandoned once Smith's guilt appeared to be far more obvious than it actually was in reality.

CHAPTER 12

Last Hours of a Young Life

The Murder of Natalie Pearman, 19–20 November 1992

Weeks before her murder, 16 year old Natalie Pearman was warned by the police that 'you are on the road to damnation'. Inspector Charles Greeney had seen Natalie at Bethel Street Police Station in Norwich when she had been picked up for prostitution. He said:

She was a waif – it was like a child dressed up as a prostitute in a short dress and cheap stockings. She looked quite pathetic. A sergeant saw her three or four weeks before her death and warned 'you will end up getting killed'. When I saw her in September I told her she was on the road to damnation – but she didn't seem to care. Her attitude was extremely hardened, bordering on the insolent. She said she had been a heroin addict but was off it now and hadn't seen her parents for a couple of years. I told her that I could offer help but I just got a blunt 'no'.

In 1990 Natalie had been a typical schoolgirl, doing well at North Walsham High School and was something of an athlete. Two years later she had become addicted to LSD and cocaine and had plummeted into the twilight world of prostitution. Her parents had seen her personality suddenly change:

She had her first sexual experience, though she hid it from us and didn't tell me until some time later. I cannot know for sure whether she was raped, or whether things just went further than she intended, but it changed her. She seemed to discover that her sexuality gave her power over the opposite sex.

Natalie had discovered drugs and worked at a burger bar in her home village of Mundesley. Her mother said:

She worked there at weekends and school holidays, and at first she spent her wages on clothes and makeup. But after a while she met people who were drug users, and things really started to go wrong. She became two people. At times she was normal, lively, aiming at a career in the army or in art. At other times she was lazy, wanting everything at once, longing for all the wrong things.

Natalie was certainly experimenting with a wide range of drugs. Her stepfather, Chris Pearman, was busy coping with his mother's terminal cancer and the family had three younger children to cope with too. Mrs Lin Pearman said:

I was desperate to help Natalie, I tried everything I could think of, but it was no good. We were at breaking point. In the end we knew that, for the sake of our sanity, our marriage and our children, we had to let Natalie go.

Just a month before her fifteenth birthday Natalie was taken into care. Lin Pearman explained: 'It was one of the hardest decisions of my life, it went against every instinct, but in my heart I knew there was no alternative.'

Two days before Natalie died she had returned home to Mundesley to collect her birth certificate because she wanted to apply for a passport so that she could travel to Europe. Her mother described this contact with her:

She rang to say she was coming and I was longing to see her and hold her. Yet when she walked in the door I was terrified. It was as though there was a thick fog of evil around her. She looked absolutely appalling, desperately ill, and dressed, as you would expect a tart to dress. My daughter was in there somewhere trying to make a bridge between us but she was petrified. She said she was going to Spain or France, because there was nothing left for her in England. Chris warned her she would either end up very, very rich or very, very dead.

Natalie's body was found at the Ringland Hills beauty spot at Easton, to the west of Norwich, at 0400 on 20 November 1992. She had been strangled.

Detective Superintendent Ron Elliott was fairly convinced that there had been a sexual motive for the attack: 'There is some evidence of disruption to clothing.'

The woodlands in the Ringland Hills area, just outside of Norwich.

In April 1993, an inquest was carried out to discover how Natalie had drifted into an underworld of drugs and prostitution. Her mother claimed that she was not given sufficient support by Social Services:

When Natalie was fourteen and we were at breaking point I turned to social services for help because we couldn't cope any longer. She was taking drugs, having underage sex and associating with criminals, and what she needed was a short, sharp shock. Social services should have put her into a home where she would have been kept away from the crowd she was mixing with. Instead they put her with foster parents and allowed her to go on seeing her so-called friends. She didn't have enough knowledge of life to be able to get herself back on the rails.

Natalie had been living with her boyfriend, Andrew Clitheroe. He had repeatedly asked her to stop working in Norwich's red light district. The inquest had learned from an unidentified man that he was her last client before she was murdered. He had had sex with her at his home and afterwards he had driven her back to the city. A few hours later a lorry driver in a roadside clearing at Ringland Hills found her body naked from the waist down.

The Coroner, James Hipwell, recorded a verdict of unlawful killing. Her boyfriend, Clitheroe, said that on the streets she was known as Maria:

I tried to get her to stop but she appeared to enjoy walking the streets. The more she went on doing it the more tarty she became. She was unable to listen to people and she always wanted to prove something.

An enormous cash reward was offered for information leading to the discovery of the murderer of Natalie Pearman. Links were made with other cases, including the murder of a West Bromwich prostitute, Samo Paul. She, too, had been strangled and had been reported missing on 4 December 1992. Detective Superintendent Dave Unwin said: 'She was a prostitute operating in the Balsall Heath area of Birmingham and even though she was a young girl, had been doing so for some considerable time.'

Police had also been looking at connections to the murder of Carol Clark, another prostitute from Gloucestershire and Karen McGregor, from Glasgow.

By January 1993 there were still twenty-four detectives working on the case. A fourth person had been arrested and then released. Stories and leads were still being followed up. Fresh clues seemed to continue to come in, but all of them led nowhere.

In 1994 psychic investigator, Carol Everett, who had worked with police on other murder enquiries, suggested further information. Everett was sure that other girls who worked as prostitutes in Norwich knew the killer. The killer, she thought, lived near Norwich, no more than twenty to thirty minutes away

The remote Ringland Hills country roads.

and that he was smart and well spoken.

Forensic tests showed that Natalie had had unprotected sex with three men in the period between the time that she was last seen alive, on the corner of Rouen Road and King Street, at 0100 on 20 November 1992 and when she was found near Taverham. Detective Inspector Bernie Kerrison said:

> *The forensic tests indicate that she had unprotected sex with someone in that short period. We have still not ever traced that person, and it is more than likely that he could have been her killer.*

Police, by October 1994, had traced and eliminated two of the three men that Natalie had been with that night. Up until that point, ten men had been arrested and later released. Three hundred blood samples had been taken; the police had also carried out 3,380 enquiries, sorted through 4,257 pieces of information and, in all, the sixty-two officers directly involved had worked 3,168 days on the case.

The police had considered that the murderer, Alan Conner, who hanged himself in August 1994, might have been Natalie's killer. He may have been responsible for six murders, twenty-two rapes and five other sex-related attacks. The police continued to search for a connection. Conner had hanged himself after murdering chambermaid, Sandra Parkinson. He had a connection with Norfolk. He had been seen in Wells in the summer of 1992. Months later, in the autumn, he had reappeared and said that he was staying in digs at Fakenham.

Natalie Pearman's murderer has never been found. As Lin Pearman said on the tenth anniversary of the discovery of her daughter's body:

> *The week before the anniversary is absolutely horrendous. By the time you get to the date you are completely washed out and I always have to take time off work because I'm not fit to think straight, let alone look after people. My other children have lived with this all their lives – Georgina was only five when it happened – it's not easy for them. There is the hope that we would know a little more about the reason why she died and that the person who did it would be brought to justice and would not be able to do it again. For ten years, whoever has done it has been leading a normal life and we have been paying the penalty for it.*

CHAPTER 13

Shadow of Fear

The Murder of Johanna Young,
23 December 1992

Fourteen year old Watton schoolgirl, Johanna Young, disappeared from her home on 23 December 1992. She was seen leaving her home in Merton Road to walk to Watton High Street on the dark and foggy night. It was 1930 and an hour later she was talking to friends on the High Street. She then walked up Norwich Road towards Griston Road and into the lane at Gillman's Drift. It was here that she probably met her murderer. She was knocked unconscious, dragged across a field and left to drown in a disused gravel pit.

There were a number of clues and key questions surrounding the case. Detectives had desperately tried to complete the jigsaw, even carrying out enquiries as far a field as France, Belgium and Holland. In all, the detectives examined 4,582 lines of enquiry. Four men were arrested but all were released without charge. Over 2,000 written statements had been taken.

The police were convinced to a large extent that the following clues could be relied upon. The murderer must have been a local or someone with local knowledge; the water filled pit was an isolated spot and was very overgrown at the time of the killing. Two people

Watton High Street.

may have been involved in moving her body, which had fractured her skull but did not kill her.

When a fingertip search of the area had taken place, Johanna's jeans were not found, yet they appeared at the murder scene on 19 January 1993. Where were these jeans between the time of her death and when they were discovered four weeks later? Equally as chilling, who had placed her trainers neatly on the verge at the top of Griston Road, where they were seen at 1030 on Christmas Eve 1992?

The police were convinced that Johanna had gone down the lane of her own accord. The actual time of death was uncertain due to the fact that her body had been in the icy water. There were footprints similar to Johanna's black trainers found in Muddy Lane. As Detective Superintendent Michael Cole, leading the hunt, said:

> Our enquiry has been aimed at Watton and has never left it. It is very likely she went down there with somebody of her own age, although not necessarily. It does not mean we narrow our sights to a killer of just her age or a bit older.

The police had never found the weapon that had fractured her skull. They were convinced it was a local killer. Cole added:

> The location of the pit indicates that someone had local knowledge of it plus the fact the killer, possibly with help, has gone back in an attempt to cover the body. It is not likely a stranger would do this.

In June 1993, the speculation that the half naked body of Johanna Young indicated a sexual motive for the attack was dismissed. The coroner, at the inquest in Dereham, Christopher Starling, said to Johanna's parents: 'Happily there was no evidence on the post mortem examination of any sexual interference with your daughter.'

An anonymous postcard was sent to Norfolk's *Evening News* offices on New Years Eve 1992. The message indicated that a youth and a girl on a motorcycle had been seen in Griston Road, Watton, at 2100 hours on 23 December. This was ninety minutes after Johanna had left home. The writer of the postcard was believed to be left-handed. Parts of the drawing contained on the postcard indicated that the motorcycle had a high front mudguard.

Johanna had been reported missing the morning after she had left the house. Reports had claimed that she had refused to talk to friends, who had called out to her that night, because she had been feeling depressed. According to her former boyfriend, Ryan Firman, Johanna had often spoken of running away from home. She had been upset when he broke up their six-month relationship shortly before her disappearance and murder:

> *We were always arguing and I wanted to cool things off for a while. She was upset but agreed with what I was saying. We thought we may get back together next month. She was a cheerful girl. We were very close and saw each other most evenings. She often said about running away to some friends who lived outside Watton, but she never told me of their names or addresses. I thought that was where she may have gone if she did not want to be found.*

Ryan had been visiting an old girlfriend at her home on the night Johanna went missing. He was obviously one of the earliest interviews police undertook and at the time of the murder there was considerable speculation about his involvement.

It is said that the police knew the identity of those who committed the crime, but still lack evidence to make an arrest.
There were also theories that drugs may have been involved. Certainly drugs were being sold in and around Johanna's school at the time. There is no serious suggestion that Johanna was taking drugs and certainly no evidence has come to light to support this.

In the weeks after the murder the usually bustling market town of Watton was quiet and subdued. Residents feared that the murderer could be amongst them. Women in particular were on edge and one local said: 'It could be someone standing next to me. I've even started carrying a bleeper in my handbag when I'm out on my own.'

The police denied that they knew who had carried out the murder. Detective Chief Inspector Peter Billingham said:

> *It's like a jigsaw puzzle. We've got the vast majority of the puzzle; we're just missing the final pieces. We don't know who did it. We've got our suspicions on lines of enquiries. We're looking for someone with a good deal of local knowledge, but we have not closed our minds to other possibilities.*

Ryan Firman continued to wear a gold chain and a ring given to him by Johanna for some time. He said a year on from the murder: 'After her funeral I knew I had to adjust to losing her.'

He had been the subject of a whispering campaign early on in the enquiry and many had suggested that he was the prime suspect. Many people shunned him, but he adamantly claimed that he had nothing to do with the killing and the police have never linked him to it, or admitted that he was a suspect. Firman said:

I'd enjoy grassing him up for what he's done, and what he's put us through. I feel bitter that nobody has been caught. I can't see how the person can keep it in – he must have told someone. By now he probably thinks he's got away with it and can carry on as normal.

He added:

I reckon she might have been coming to see me. I have been worried – I thought something might have happened but was trying not to believe it.

Firman had not been aware that Johanna had been killed until the local press had told him on 27 December.

Johanna had been described as a happy go lucky girl, friendly and with not a care in the world. When she had asked to go out that evening she had seemed full of life and cheerful. She had visited Norwich a few days earlier to buy clothes especially for Christmas Day. When she had gone out her parents had thought that it was a spur of the moment decision for her not to return home, as she had taken no extra clothes or money with her. Oddly, and still unexplained, is the fact that Johanna had fixed fifty Christmas cards to her bedroom wall. When her parents checked to see if she had come home, they found she had taken them down and put them in a box on top of her wardrobe.

What is not clear about the exact nature of her rendezvous with her murderer is why she walked down that lonely lane on a dark, foggy night. Why were her clothes strewn all over the area? Her tights and underwear were found draped on bushes by a path near the pit. Her jeans had disappeared and then miraculously reappeared and her trainers had been placed on a verge.

The police did suggest one theory, that Johanna's death could have been as the result of a prank and in fact her murder had been nothing more than an accident. There continues to be much rumour and speculation surrounding the case. It may never be known what was on her mind or where she had intended to go.

Did the killer have an accomplice? If so, what was the reason for that accomplice still remaining silent after all these years? The police remain convinced that the killer was local, because of where the body was found. Whether this was a false assumption or not may never be known.

CHAPTER 14

The Killer Could Strike Again

The Murder of Ron Cousins, 16 April 1994

I n 2003 the Essex Police's Investigative Review Team was set up to look at ten unresolved cases in the Essex area. Some of them dated back thirty years. One perplexing and seemingly motiveless murder, with a bizarre signature, dated back to 1994. Whatever the motive for the killing of 78 year old Ron Cousins, it was not robbery.

Ron Cousins was found in his home in Anchor Street, Chelmsford. He had been strangled, and he had multiple stab wounds. The circumstances in which the body was left were altogether inexplicable and macabre. For one thing a tin of white emulsion paint had been thrown over him and the murderer or murderers had stuffed pages from the family bible into his mouth. A knife from Ron Cousins' own scullery, which was not the murder weapon, had been placed on his body. The tiny mid-terrace house had been completely ransacked; there were several knives lying around the place and it was clear to the police that whoever had killed the pensioner had been in the house for some time. What they could not be sure about was whether they were

Anchor Street, Chelmsford.

there after the killing or whether Ron Cousins had still been alive while his house was being turned upside down.

Neighbours were alerted to the house at around 1000 hours on Saturday, 16 April 1994. Ron Cousins' curtains were still pulled and it appeared that a bath was overflowing, as there was water pouring from the outflow pipe of his bathroom.

Detective Chief Inspector Kevin Macey led the case and it was his opinion that Ron Cousins knew his killer or killers. What was as chilling was that the psychological profiles that had been drawn up indicated that there was a high probability that this would happen again. Macey speculated that the bath was overfilling because the killer or killers had washed after murdering Ron Cousins. Speaking in 1999, five years after he said:

> *I believe he would have had blood and paint on him. The person responsible has been harbouring a terrible secret for five years. It is possible that someone known to the killer has been suffering the anguish of sharing that secret and not coming forward to unburden themselves. Anyone capable of doing what was done to a vulnerable old man like Mr Cousins must be apprehended.*

Human hair and partial fingerprints had been taken shortly after the discovery of the body and these were being re-examined as new forensic techniques became available.

Ron Cousins was a devout Christian and certainly the crime had horrified local people at the time. When the police launched an appeal on the fifth anniversary of the murder they received just one call in response. A police spokesman said:

> *Unfortunately I think that witness was giving us information we already had but the enquiries are going to continue and we are still carrying out the DNA testing.*

The police admitted that this was a disappointing response, but five years had indeed passed:

> *But then again we did have a very good response right at the start and it may well be that we have exhausted that line of enquiry. This was not a setback to the enquiry, it will continue and we do have the forensic testing to concentrate on.*

The police reconfirmed the fact that robbery did not seem to have been the motive. In fact £700 in cash had been found in the house. Nothing else appeared to have been stolen, despite the fact that every room had been ransacked. The knife that had been used to stab Ron Cousins had never been traced.

The only major lead that the police still had was the sighting of a man on Friday, 15 April. Several witnesses had seen him standing outside Ron Cousins' house for around two and a half hours on that day. Witnesses described him as being in his early twenties, around 5 feet 8 inches tall and with blonde hair.

The police were firmly of the opinion that the murderer was a local person, but even the DNA testing that had taken place in 1999 led them nowhere and no further progress was made. Around 2,000 people had been interviewed about the murder, but nothing emerged.

Suddenly, six years later in April 2005 three people were arrested. There were two men, one aged 52 and the other aged 56. They had been arrested on suspicion of murder. The third person, a woman aged 57, was being questioned on suspicion of perverting the course of justice. It seemed for a while that the cold case investigation team had finally turned up viable suspects that the initial enquiries had failed to reveal. A few days passed and then there was the news that the three people had been released without charge.

The case, of course, remains open. As the trail gets colder and colder and the initiatives yield ever-decreasing numbers of responses from the public, some wonder whether the killer or killers will ever be found.

A view up Anchor Street, towards the Chelmsford town centre.

CHAPTER 15

Was There A Motive?

The Death of Carol Tucker, 21 July 1995

Nick Tucker had twenty-eight years' service with the Royal Air Force and had attained the rank of squadron leader. But in November 1999, by a majority of ten to two, he was convicted of murdering his wife. He was sentenced to life imprisonment. To this day many people believe that this was a dreadful miscarriage of justice.

It was Friday, 21 July 1995 and Tucker and his wife had just eaten a meal at the Red Lion pub in Icklingham in Suffolk.

*The Red Lion in Icklingham where Carole and Nick Tucker
had their last meal together.*

Carol had had some wine with her meal, so Nick was driving. Nick was just back from six months' military service in Croatia and Carol had just finished her last day at work.

In their Ford car they were driving towards a bridge at Lackford. Nick would later claim that he saw two deer on the road and that he had to swerve to avoid them. The car left the road and plunged into the water of the River Lark. This would have been around 2230. A fisherman heard tyres screech, a car skid and then a thump.

Five minutes after a cyclist, William Barber, saw the part-submerged car in the water. There was no one to be seen so he cycled back to a nearby house and raised the alarm. It was now 2246. Barber managed to flag down a motorist, James Woods, and they went together to investigate. Woods heard muffled breathing from under the water and they found Nick Tucker in the river. He was bleeding from the head and seemed to be unconscious. They pulled him to the bank, with Tucker drifting in and out of consciousness.

The deserted scene was soon full of people; other motorists stopped, the police and an ambulance arrived. One of the police, PC Paul Dewing, saw something red floating under the bridge. They retrieved the 15-stone Carol Tucker. Attempts at resuscitation were made and when a doctor arrived on the scene

The River Lark, scene of the death of Carole Tucker.

she was pronounced dead.

Nick Tucker was taken to West Suffolk Hospital and arrived there at 2345. After being given treatment for his head wound he was sent home at 0105 the following morning when he told his two teenage children that their mother had died.

Initially the police believed it was a straightforward road traffic accident, with nothing suspicious. Paradoxically it was Nick Tucker himself that caused the police to have suspicions. He could not believe that his wife had drowned in eighteen inches of water. The police then began to wonder why the car had not suffered a great deal of damage and how a minor accident could have led to the death of Carol Tucker.

Another query appeared when the pub's till roll showed that the Tuckers had paid their bill and left at 2120. Since the accident scene was only a few minutes' drive away from the pub, what had happened in the intervening hour? The police dug around Nick Tucker's background and discovered that he had been having an affair with a Serbian interpreter while he was serving in Croatia.

The court would later be told that there were abrasions under Carol's left arm and there were bruises on her left breast. The prosecution maintained that these were consistent injuries with Carol being held under water. There were also abrasions on Carol's back, which the prosecution suggested were caused when Nick Tucker pulled her out of the car. There were also haemorrhages on the inner lining of her eyelids. The pathologist, Dr David Harrison, had never come across these injuries in cases of drowning. It was his opinion that they were associated with strangulation. The cause of death was drowning and according to the prosecution Tucker had staged the accident, pulled his wife out of the car and then killed her.

An expert witness from Addenbrooke's Hospital maintained that the injuries to Nick Tucker's head would not have caused unconsciousness. Carefully the prosecution had put together a case that seemed to point towards Nick Tucker's guilt.

Lieutenant Tim Stear had spent a month with Tucker in Croatia. He described Tucker as being like a lap dog as far as his alleged Serbian mistress, Dijana Dudukovic, was concerned. Another witness, Bernard Du Pasquier, a Swiss official who had helped Dudukovic escape to Zurich told the court that after Carol's death Nick Tucker had written to Dudukovic, telling her that he loved her. The Swiss also claimed that Tucker had telephoned her sometimes twice a day. In November 1995 it had been Tucker that had booked and paid for Dudukovic's flight from Belgrade to Zurich.

What had appeared to be a fairly flimsy case now seemed to produce a definite motive. Nick Tucker had been charged with the murder in March 1996 and had been remanded in custody. He was later granted bail and remained free throughout the trial, until he was convicted in November 1997. There were enormous holes in the case against him.

The first problem was the cause of death. In fact according to the Home Office pathologist, Dr Harrison, the cause of death was heart stoppage as a result of drowning. Another expert, Dr West, was of the opinion that death had been caused because Carol had choked on food. A Dr Cary supported Dr Harrison's assessment, but a Professor Knight could not determine the cause of death. There had been a second coroner's inquest to determine the cause of death, but this was no more conclusive than the first. What transpired in court was that barristers argued about the cause of death, rather than its definite cause being determined by pathologists.

Given the fact that there was divided opinion as to whether Carol Tucker was murdered or not, there was still a problem as to whether or not she had died in an accident. It seems that the jury convicted Tucker because they dismissed his account of the events leading up to the incident.

According to the police the impact speed of the car was 10 mph. The car was not badly damaged and there was the question as to whether Nick Tucker was play-acting as far as his head injury was concerned. There was another issue about the particular car. It was from a batch that had a recognized seatbelt fault. In fact Ford recalled this batch of vehicles.

Given that Carol Tucker was overweight, the seatbelt would have been too loose for Nick Tucker, as it was fitted with a clip device. This would have made it more possible that he had struck his head on the interior of the vehicle. Mr Justice Gage, the presiding judge, told the jurors in his summing up:

When he [Tucker] was seen by witnesses following it [the incident], he was simply play-acting. Either he was not rendered unconscious at all or, if he was, it was only for a few minutes.

This was one of the decisive points, as an expert in emergency care told the court that he believed Tucker was initially unconscious and the witnesses saw him beginning to come round.

The other important issue was the missing hour. Nick Tucker claimed that they were still in the pub at 2200. Why then was the bill calculated and timed at 2120? It is believed that the till had probably not been adjusted when British Summertime came into effect, hence the supposed missing hour.

The same stretch of road had been the scene of 119 accidents between 1990 and shortly after the death of Carol Tucker, which prompted the council to improve the road conditions.

Four weeks after the crash, on the same day that Nick Tucker was arrested on suspicion of murder, he was admitted to hospital, where he was diagnosed as suffering from depression and post-traumatic stress disorder.

In the end the jury were out for over seven hours and Nick Tucker was convicted by a majority verdict and sentenced to life. He lost an appeal in December 1998, even though the Appeal Court judges conceded that there was no direct evidence suggesting that he had murdered his wife.

During the trial Tucker had become involved with another woman, Jenny Peacock, who has supported him throughout, even when in 2002 Tucker was told he would not be granted a new appeal. Meanwhile Nick Tucker waits, hoping that the Criminal Case Review Commission will refer his case to the Court of Appeal. Supporters, including Martin Bell and Terry Waite, are convinced of Nick Tucker's innocence. Several pathologists and experts have reinvestigated the forensic evidence and all so far have concluded that there is no pathological evidence to suggest that Carol Tucker was strangled or strangled to the point of unconsciousness so that her husband could drown her.

In an interview with BBC Radio Suffolk in March 2004, Professor Derrick Pounder, an independent opinion, said:

The evidence that was presented at trial was very misleading indeed. The prosecution raised the issue of strangulation for which there was no medical evidence whatsoever, and of course having raised it would have prejudiced the minds of the jury. It's quite remarkable to have a conviction for murder where there is no medical evidence of murder.

CHAPTER 16

Fuelled by Rumour

The Murder of Gary Chick, 18 November 1996

In December 1999 a 28 year old postman, Paul Rowley, found himself accused, charged and facing a trial for the murder of a 40 year old man. The offence had allegedly taken place at 0250 on 18 November 1996. The victim was Gary Chick, a bouncer, and he had been attacked on the seafront near Clacton Pier by a group of masked men. The only witness to the attack was Chick's girlfriend, Rosalind Vaughan.

The gang had walked behind the couple, close to the Memorial Gardens, and had then smashed Gary Chick over the head with a metal or wooden pole. The group of men ran off, laughing and joking, before they sped away in a waiting car.

Gary Chick was a doorman, a father of three and described by his friends and family as a gentle giant. He lived in Clacton and worked at the town's Tom Pepper's Club in Pier Avenue. He was off duty at the time of the attack.

The man facing the charges in 1999 was a man who was said to have been a regular at the club, but had been refused entry on two occasions in the past, due to his rowdy behaviour.

Gary Chick and his girlfriend had gone to the Waverley Hall Hotel on the night of the attack. They spent about an hour there and then left to take a walk along the seafront. It was alleged that Rowley and two others were trailing them. The prosecuting counsel, Howard Godfrey QC, said:

Miss Vaughan was aware that there was a group of people behind them. She then became aware of the people running up behind her and her fiancé and it was a group of three men. Without warning the first man hit Mr Chick on the back of the head with an object and Mr Chick fell straight to the ground. When he fell, the two other men each hit him

*on the side of the head and after the first hit the other two
young men pulled dark woollen hats over their faces.*

In court Godfrey made an admission:

*The prosecution cannot say that it was Mr Rowley who
inflicted the fatal blow. But we do say he was part of a team
of three people who approached Mr Chick, armed with
weapons of some sort, intending to either kill him or cause
really serious harm.*

In fact Rowley had been up to no good earlier in the
evening. The police had arrested him for making lewd
gestures at them. The police drove him home and they told
him that he could return to the seafront provided he
behaved himself. The police had arrested and questioned
him back in December 1996, but he had not been charged.
When Rowley was arrested the police found a dark, woollen
hat in his car.

The only witness to the attack was Rosalind Vaughan. She
told the court:

*I was aware there were other people around when we
were in the sunken garden. I could hear laughing and
voices then as we got to the end of the path, I was aware
that suddenly the people were right on top of us. I was
holding Gary's right arm and was suddenly aware of a
tall person jumping around, leaping up, and reaching
across the front of Gary's head. Then Gary fell forward
and I turned round and there were three people there.
They stood back at first, and they had woollen hats and
I saw a face and they pulled their hats down. They went
forward and they each hit Gary across the head with
something like a cosh. They didn't speak, after he had
been attacked they ran off laughing.*

Unbeknown to the prosecution the case was about to fall
apart. In an original statement she had made to the police
Vaughan had claimed that there were four attackers and that
she had not named Rowley as one of the attackers initially,
but had later. She admitted that she could not identify the
first attacker and was not sure whether or not it was Rowley.
To explain herself she said:

That was the day of the murder. My head was not exactly working properly. I was in a state of shock.

Judge Fabian Evans, presiding over the case in Middlesex Guildhall Crown Court, ruled that Rosalind Vaughan's evidence had 'many flaws'. She had told the court that she recognized Rowley as one of the men who had attacked her boyfriend. Then she had changed her version of the incident. She had originally claimed there were four attackers and, in fact, had not identified Rowley until two years later. As Judge Evans commented:

There is no clear picture of what happened, and you cannot use the evidence of Miss Vaughan to assist. Her opportunity of seeing his features at that time was very limited – the lighting was poor, and the incident must have been over in seconds. She could only have had a fleeting glance of the attacker's face.

The judge was also concerned about the objectivity of the evidence being presented as the true account of events by Miss Vaughan:

She seems to have expressed vindictive views during the course of the case, perhaps to coincide with the arrest of a man and woman during the investigation. Someone killed Gary Chick. You may think that somebody murdered him, but this case reeks of suspicion and may well have been fuelled by rumour.

With that the judge instructed the jury to find Paul Rowley, a father of one and Royal Mail van driver, not guilty. Rowley had always claimed that he was in bed at the time of the attack. He admitted that he had been at the Waverley Hall Hotel, where Gary Chick and Rosalind Vaughan had been drinking that evening. He claimed that he had left the hotel and gone home. He refused to comment to the press after being released.

The murder of Gary Chick had received an enormous amount of publicity around Essex and it was a case that could not be forgotten by people in the Clacton area. As if the murder itself were not enough to devastate the Chick family, the fact that the only person that had been charged with the murder was acquitted had devastated them even further. Joyce Chick, Gary's mother, said:

> *It's terrible, every day I dust his photo and I kiss him every morning and every night before I go to bed. I still can't believe it, when I think those animals are out there walking about and we are suffering.*

Joyce Chick begged for someone to come forward:

> *They must have mothers and sons, surely when they think about it how can they sleep when they know they have killed somebody in cold blood? I hope they get them before I die. It's a nightmare for me, I miss him so much.*

Seven years after the killing the case was still open. Jenny Chick, one of Gary's daughters, said:

> *It is seven years since my father was murdered and not a day goes by without us thinking of him. You hope it will get easier after time but if anything it is harder now we are older. Laura [her sister and one of Gary's other daughters] and I are now married and although we tried to enjoy the weddings we couldn't help but feel sad that Dad couldn't be there. It is all so heartbreaking that he will never get to meet my son or Roxanne's [Gary's remaining daughter] daughter. We all still miss him so much and will never be able to rest until those responsible for my father's brutal murder are brought to justice.*

Ten years after the murder the case still remained open and although there had not been any further breakthroughs to identify the assailants of the 'gentle giant', the police once again renewed their appeal. A spokesman at the time said: 'The passage of time makes it no less important that Mr Chick's attackers are brought to justice.'

The case remains open and Essex police still hope to receive the breakthrough call that both they and the family have been waiting for, for so long.

CHAPTER 17

Undiluted Evil

The Murder of Vicky Hall, September 1999

The immediate area between Ipswich and Felixstowe is now more closely associated in our subconscious with the five Ipswich prostitute murders that hit the headlines in 2006. However, in September 2000 the regional press were no less animated about a case that had come up a year before. The *Evening Star* in Ipswich, on the first anniversary of the murder had posted a £25,000 reward. The police hoped that the reward would finally flush out the killer.

Victoria (Vicky) Hall was just 17 when she went missing at around 0230 on Sunday, 19 September 1999. She had spent the

The Band Box nightclub in Felixstowe.

night out in Felixstowe with her friend, Gemma Algar. They had been to the Bandbox nightclub and then bought a kebab to eat on the way home. The girls walked towards their homes in Trimley St Mary, only a short distance from the centre of Felixstowe.

Vicky and Gemma parted company at the junction of High Road and Faulkeners Way in Trimley St Mary. Faulkeners Way was Vicky's intended destination, but she never made it home. Vicky was a tiny, 5 feet 1 inch tall girl with blonde hair and blue eyes. At the time she was wearing a short black dress, a brown jacket and platform or high-heeled black sandals. She was also carrying a tiny half-moon shaped black purse. At first the disappearance was treated as abduction. The police had already established that there was a car with a loud exhaust in the area at the time she went missing. More chillingly, local residents had heard screams in the early hours of the morning.

Only the week before a 19 year old girl had been raped after spending an evening at the club. Vicky's father, Graham, said on 20 September 1999:

> *We can only sit and wait – we have contacted all our relatives and friends but nobody has seen Vicky. She likes to go out to clubs but she is really a quiet girl and does not drink. We were worried about her following last week's rape and we urged her to get a taxi home or we would go and collect her. Perhaps if she had been in the habit of staying out we would have been more relaxed about it. But she has never stayed out. She is supposed to call me when she is going to leave and get a taxi home but she did not phone. I dropped off to sleep and when we woke she was not here.*

Vicky's parents had contacted the police as soon as they realized their daughter had not arrived home. There was no sign that Vicky had planned to run away; all of her clothes and money were still in her room. Claire Taylor, Vicky's aunt, added:

> *Vicky is a sensible and reliable girl who always tells her parents where she is going and when she will be back. She has one close friend who she would certainly have confided in if anything was wrong and she spent all day with her on Saturday. She does not have a boyfriend and is not in trouble at school.*

The two senior investigating officers, Detective Superintendent

Roy Lambert and Detective Chief Inspector Mick Warden, were concerned for Vicky's safety. There appeared to be no reason why she had disappeared. Lambert said:

As time passes our concern for her safety is obviously growing. We are trying to establish the exact route Vicky may have taken.

Warden added:

When Vicky separated from her friend she was only about three minutes' walk from home. The area she had to walk through is part of a housing estate, but no one has reported hearing or seeing anything suspicious in the area.

This was, of course, just before residents came forward to report hearing screams and a car speeding off.

The next day Lambert confirmed that the police had received over eighty telephone calls. Many people had not got in contact with the police straight away, as they just believed that they had heard children or teenagers being boisterous. Lambert made another appeal:

We urgently need to hear from anyone who was in the area during the early hours of Sunday morning – particularly anyone who may have seen Vicky or a car, which may have had a particularly loud exhaust. I cannot rule out the possibility that there is another explanation for her disappearance but one can only interpret the screams as suggesting there was some violence subjected to her or she has been abducted against her will.

The final part of Vicky's journey after she had left Gemma would have taken precisely three minutes and twelve seconds. Something seriously wrong occurred during that short period of time.

On 23 September the son of a former professional footballer was arrested in connection with the disappearance. The man had been one of Vicky's former boyfriends and he was arrested at 0525 in the morning in Ipswich. On the same day he was released without charge. The police were also carrying out house-to-house enquiries in Trimley St Mary.

Tragically, on 24 September Vicky's body was found. She

Faulkeners Way, Trimley St Mary.

was naked in a water filled ditch around twenty-five miles from her home. A post mortem examination had proved inconclusive and there were no obvious signs of cause of death. There was speculation that she had either been suffocated or strangled. The police also discovered a burned out car around a mile from where Vicky's body had been found. Tests were underway to see if there was any link.

Police were waiting for the results of forensic tests to see if Vicky had been sexually assaulted. Lambert admitted that the fact that the body had been found naked could suggest there had been a sexual motive. The post mortem examination showed that she had not been the victim of a sexual assault and there was confirmation that she had either been strangled or suffocated. A man walking his dog had found the body, but despite a comprehensive search of the immediate area the police could not find any of Vicky's clothes.

Prayers were said for Vicky at a church in Trimley St Mary. The local vicar, the Reverend Rod Corke, said that the local community was 'hurt and broken' by the 'undiluted evil' that had taken away a 'bright, vivacious young lady'. Despite the fact that Vicky's family had feared the worst, it was still a dreadful shock when their worst fears came true. Reverend Corke had visited Vicky's parents several times over the weekend after the body had been found on the Friday:

> *Considering what they have gone through they are bearing up well. But they are devastated. No one can imagine what it must have been like for them over the past week.*

The man that found the body had not walked his dog along that route for several weeks. It was a rarely used bridle path, next to which was the ditch where Vicky's body had been dumped. The dog walker said:

> *I'd only gone a few yards when my dog started growling at something in the water. I called her away. She was reluctant to go, which is very unusual. Some relatives were with us for the weekend and I told them what I had seen, that there was something strange about it. We decided we ought to take another look. I had not walked this particular bridle path for some time because it was wet. It is possible Vicky was there from the Sunday.*

There was no obvious link between the burned out car and the ditch where the body was found. As far as the police were concerned: 'Anyone who attempted to walk between the two places would have had to cover over a mile of farmland and would probably have been covered in mud.'

The car, a red Subaru estate, had been sold by a garage in South Yorkshire to a man who had given his name as Sanderson.

Investigations continued throughout 1999 and in January 2000 the police announced the arrest of two men and a woman, all in their early twenties. Two of them were girlfriend and boyfriend, who came from Vicky's home village of Trimley St Mary. They had been arrested for conspiring to pervert the course of justice. The other man, aged 22, was being held on suspicion of murder. Very quickly the three people were released without charge. They were all believed to have lived on or close to the route that Vicky had taken once she had left Gemma.

There was another sensational arrest and charges, this time against a young businessman in his mid-twenties. He appeared before magistrates in Ipswich and asked permission for his release on bail pending trial. This was turned down. The essential link, as far as Michael Lawson QC, the prosecutor, was

concerned was that grains of soil matching mud from the area
near the water filled ditch were found on the accelerator of the
accused man's car. Speaking through his solicitor, a statement
said: 'He totally denies any involvement in the offence and will
strenuously deny his guilt.'

Lawson said:

> *There is little doubt she* [Vicky] *must have been abducted
> from the scene shortly after she departed from her friend. We
> shall never know why. Whether it was an argument or a
> struggle that had fatal consequences or whether it was
> something else.*

The case was underway in November 2001. Gemma Algar
described the last moments she spent with Vicky before they
parted at the High Road junction:

> *We were chatting then Vicky said she would phone me when
> she got up next morning. Then she walked off and I crossed
> the road.*

About three minutes later Gemma heard a scream:

> *It was two high-pitched screams – female – just a few seconds
> gap between them. They came from the housing estate. I
> thought it was somebody larking about.*

Gemma went on to tell the jury, of seven men and five women,
that she had become friends with Vicky at Orwell High School:

> *I spoke to her every day. If I didn't see her, I would speak to
> her on the telephone. She was caring. She always had a smile
> on her face. Happy. She was always there for you if you needed
> someone to talk to. Always made time for you.*

The prosecution claimed that the accused man had gone on a
pub-crawl in Felixstowe and had ended up at the Bandbox
Club. He had then taken a taxi to Trimley St Mary, arriving
there at approximately the same time as the two girls reached
the village. He had then, they claimed, abducted Vicky in his car.

The two-week trial at Norwich Crown Court ended in
spectacular fashion. The key part of the prosecution's case was
the fact that the soil found in the accused man's car was

'strikingly similar' to the soil at the site where Vicky's body had been found. However, the defence had brought forward an expert witness. He told the court that similar soil was found across East Anglia. The damning part was that the high uranium content actually indicated that the soil found in the car had not come from the murder scene.

When the jury went out to consider their verdict they deliberated for just ninety minutes. They returned to court and pronounced a unanimous not guilty verdict. Throughout the accused man had protested his innocence. He had neither met Vicky nor did he recognize the photographs of her.
Outside the court he said:

> *I would like to thank my family and friends and my girlfriend for standing by me and never doubting me for a second. Obviously my sympathies go out to Vicky Hall's family. I am relieved it is all over and I was confident this would be the result. A jury of twelve normal members of the public have reached the verdict. I had confidence in myself. I did not commit this crime. I am innocent.*

The accused man had spent nearly a year of his life in prison. He was understandably relieved that it was all over.

It may have been over for him, but the nightmare would continue for the Hall family. As Graham Hall said:

Felixstowe seafront at dusk.

In a way we were expecting this verdict especially when the jury returned so quickly. Whether [he] *was found guilty or not really made very little difference to us. Unless someone actually owns up to their actions on the night and tells us exactly what happened, that is the only little bit of help we could have.*

Gemma Algar added:

We have been going to court for the last ten days to try to find out what happened to Vicky after I said goodnight to her. The attacker will never know how much pain he has caused to Vicky's family and will never feel as terrified as Vicky probably felt that night. The last two years have been very up and down emotionally for me as I have tried to get my head around what has happened. I have had so much support from my family, friends and police and I would like to thank them all. I hope one day someone will own up to their actions. I still think about her a lot. I remember her smile. This is a sad day.

The police had no other option but to continue their enquiries. During the investigation so far thousands of people had been interviewed and dozens had been arrested. As far as the police were concerned the hunt would go on. As Lorinda Hall, Vicky's mother, said at a memorial service shortly after the discovery of her daughter's body:

Victoria was as perfect as everybody says. We will miss her terribly. Our lives will never be the same and her death left a hole in our lives which will never be filled.

At its height 100 officers were investigating the case. The police followed up 12,000 lines of enquiry and received over 3,000 pieces of information from the public. Detective Superintendent Roy Lambert said of the case:

Victoria's murder sparked off one of the biggest investigations undertaken by Suffolk police. The public support we received was extraordinary and I would like to thank the thousands of people who offered their help and information. Any new information or leads which come in will be fully investigated so I would appeal to anyone out there who may know anything about this incident to contact the police.

CHAPTER 18

Covered in Blood

The Murder of Ronald Fuller, 29 August 2000

It was 0745 on Tuesday, 29 August 2000 and painter and decorator Ronald Fuller was leaving his home in Parkside, Grays, in Essex. Ronald Fuller had a chequered background. He had been a doorman at the Epping Forest Country Club. Following an incident a man had died there and Ronald had been arrested for public order offences.

On the morning in question Ronald was approached by a man who was described as being white, slim, of athletic build, with mousy hair and around 5 feet 7 inches tall. He was wearing a leather three-quarter length jacket with a belt, dark trousers, boots and gloves. His crash helmet had a predominantly black and yellow pattern on it. He had stepped off a scooter with VMX as part of its number plate. It was also showing a learner's plate.

Four shots rang out and Ronald Fuller fell to the ground. The assailant got back onto his scooter and sped off towards the old A13, via King Edward Drive.

Ronald's common law wife, Larissa Tuitt, ran screaming from their bungalow. Ronald was rushed to Basildon Hospital, where he died forty minutes after the attack, without regaining consciousness. It seemed immediately apparent that this was no chance encounter, neither was this a robbery that had gone tragically wrong. The assailant had clearly meant to target Ronald Fuller and execute him gangland style. Ronald had died from two shots to his head and two shots into his body from a 9mm gun.

Armed police immediately sealed off the area and a police spokesman confirmed:

A number of shots were heard and a man was seen to leave the area on what is described as a motor scooter with some chrome on it. We are anxious to speak to anyone who may have heard or seen anything at the time in the area, particularly in respect of the motorcycle.

Ronald Fuller, Larissa and their young son had only moved into the area two months beforehand. A neighbour, Ann Pryke, told reporters:

> *I was upstairs and I heard three shots, I went to the front door and heard the girlfriend screaming so I ran to help. But there wasn't anything I could do. He was covered in blood and obviously dying.*

Despite intense police activity, a month or more passed without any significant breakthrough. The neighbours on Parkside were still terrified that such a vicious attack had taken place in the quiet, suburban street. One of the neighbours said:

> *Until the killer is found and locked up, none of us will feel truly safe. It has left everybody shocked and bewildered that something like that can happen in such a quiet, ordinary neighbourhood. The feeling it has left everyone is one of bewilderment more than anything, although some people are worried that house prices in the street might have been affected.*

In November there was another major incident. A man from Billericay, Kenny Beagle, also known as Kenneth Kenny, was shot three times in the head at point blank range, as he waited beside a ticket machine in the grounds of Oldchurch Hospital, Romford. He died in less than an hour. Two men were seen running from the car park wearing hoods and scarves.

Beagle was well known to the police and had a string of criminal convictions. Immediately parallels were drawn between the two cold-blooded killings. As police said:

> *There are too many similarities between the two shootings for us not to look at them together. We have yet to catch anyone for the Fuller murder and there may be some kind of link. Until we look at both carefully we won't know. These shootings happened a few miles apart and both bore the hallmarks of professional hits.*

The police were as baffled with this case as they were with Fuller's execution. Detective Inspector Cliff Haines of Essex police's major investigation team said of the Fuller case:

We are still pursuing a lot of leads, and remain hopeful that we will catch the killer. It will take time, but we are confident that we will get to the bottom of this.

As for one of the neighbours of Ronald Fuller in Parkside, it was all appearing to look rather too dangerous and murky: 'I don't know why he was shot and I don't want to know.'

The police discovered that Beagle had been lured to the hospital car park after receiving a telephone call to his home in Billericay. The police admitted that they were unable to establish a motive for the execution, despite the fact that thirty officers were working solely on this case. Detective Inspector Brian Sweeting of the Serious Crime Group said: 'He was clearly called to this meeting and not for any other purpose than for these people to kill him.'

A staff nurse was driving out of the car park when the gunshots were fired. She said: 'I've never heard a gun, except on television, but my gut feeling was "it's a gunshot". It was quite loud, quite piercing.'

Many involved in looking at Essex crime believe that these two killings were just another round in the violence between opposing Essex gangs. Back in 1995 Tony Tucker, Craig Rolfe and Patrick Tate were all shot dead as they sat in their Range Rover. This famous case was known as the Rettendon Triple Murders.

There were parallels, as Kenneth Beagle was believed to be involved in drug dealing and kidnapping. The three men murdered in the Range Rover had been supplying ecstasy and three young people had died as a result of taking the drug. Such was the competition to supply drugs that many people were maimed or beaten during this period. Two men were given triple life sentences for the murders of the men in the Range Rover. But there is, apparently, even some doubt as to whether the two men convicted of the murders were even involved.

There were many that believed that the Ronald Fuller case was definitely linked to incidents that had happened outside the Epping Forest Country Club. The police never ruled out the possibility that this was the case. The day before Ronald Fuller's murder, two bouncers were shot at the same club. One was shot in the back and the other in the stomach. They were trying to stop a fight between two men who had been thrown out of the club.

The police eventually came round to the opinion that a contract had been put out on Ronald Fuller, after he had been implicated in the stabbing of Darren Pearman at the same club in the previous October. Concerned that any such link would escalate the situation, the police quickly released a rebuttal that this was their line of enquiry. Many thought the police were continuing to follow that line of enquiry.

What was of particular interest was the ammunition that had been used in Fuller's killing. The police said:

> *The ammunition used – 9mm cartridges – is a fairly standard size which both the police and the armed forces use. Handguns using this kind of ammunition were withdrawn from use under the government scheme following the Dunblane shootings, but obviously there are some still currently with the criminal fraternity.*

As far as the owner of the country club, Peter Pomfrett, was concerned, he was aghast at the fact that the media had painted his club as a haunt of criminals and gangsters. The club had 30,000 members and he was adamant that the club security was stringent. The police continued to believe that there was no link between any of the incidents at the club and Fuller's murder. Detective Inspector Len Jarman said:

> *There is no reason to link this matter with any other incidents taking place in any other parts of Essex or Herts. This was an isolated incident.*

Years later the basic information about the Ronald Fuller case can still be found on the Essex Police website. It is one of the ten major undetected Essex murder cases. An Investigative Review Team has identified the cases and £5,000 has been offered to assist in solving of any of them. Despite the fact that the Fuller case has a cold trail, the head of the Investigative Review Team, Detective Superintendent Simon Coxall, said:

> *Cases of this seriousness will never be put to rest, and Essex police will continue to do all that is possible to bring the offenders involved to justice and continue to make Essex a safe place where criminals will always have to look over their shoulder and await that knock on the door.*

CHAPTER 19

No Pathological Evidence

The Murder of Jacqueline Tindsley, March 2002 and Joan Albert, 16 December 2001

In November 2002 Steven Puaca was convicted of murdering his partner, Jacqueline Tindsley. She had been suffocated in their home in Lowestoft, Suffolk. The key part of the evidence revolved around testimony given by Dr Michael Heath. He was a pathologist and had stated that the victim had been smothered while on her bed. Two other pathologists gave an alternative view of the cause of death. They believed that she had probably died from an epileptic seizure, which had been brought on by a drugs overdose.

Jacqueline was 55 at the time of her death and Steven Puaca would spend three years in prison, before an Appeals Court ruled on his conviction.

It had been Dr Heath's contention that Jacqueline had been smothered in the bed of their Lowestoft flat. Two defence pathologists, backed up by five other pathologists, concluded that there was no pathological evidence for that conclusion.

Jacqueline had been found lying facedown in a foetal position on her bed. Dr Heath had claimed that the murderer had pushed her face into the bed. The Appeal Court Judge Lord Justice Hooper, said of this: 'We confess to a certain surprise that the deceased could have been suffocated in this way, but that was the evidence which Dr Heath gave.'

It had been proven that Jacqueline Tindsley was a heavy drinker and that she already had a history of drug overdoses. Post mortem tests on her showed that she had taken five different prescription drugs. One of these was at a level associated with fatalities.

Originally, the defence had called the two pathologists that had given the cause of death as a drug overdose and fit, as opposed to smothering. Lord Justice Hooper said of their evidence:

They did not, however, rule out the possibility of smothering. But what they did say, and say most forcefully, was that there was no pathological evidence to support Dr Heath's view. They have subsequently had the backing of five further pathologists who either gave evidence before us at the request of the appellant, or who provided reports, which were before us. Those pathologists said they would not have given suffocation as the cause of death. They strongly challenged a number of matters on which Dr Heath relied in order to reach his conclusion.

Lord Justice Hooper went on to say that this was a case:

In which the evidence at trial, the manner in which the trial proceeded and the fresh evidence which we have received leave us wholly satisfied that the conviction must be regarded as unsafe.

Consequently, the 38 year old Steven Puaca was freed on appeal. His solicitor, Chris Brown, said: 'He is very pleased, but he is also understandably sad that he has been accused of what he was accused of and that he has carried the stigma for three and a half years.'

This was not the only case that directly involved Dr Heath. He was the pathologist that conducted the examinations in the murders of Lin and Megan Russell, and the death of Stuart Lubbock, who had been found in the swimming pool of Michael Barrymore's home in Harlow in March 2001.

On the eve of a hearing to consider Dr Heath's position, he resigned. Some twenty disciplinary charges had, at that stage, been upheld against him. The advisory board for forensic pathology believed that his conduct brought into question his fitness to practise.

Significantly, as far as unsolved cases in East Anglia are concerned, this also affects the murder of Joan Albert in Capel St Mary. The accused man, Simon Hall, was jailed for life in 2003.

Seventy-nine year old Joan Albert was found stabbed to death in her hallway of her Capel St Mary home on 16 December 2001. The police believed that she had been repeatedly stabbed, after having disturbed a burglar. There were signs that an intruder had broken into the house via a rear window. At the time Detective Superintendent Roy Lambert of Suffolk police said: 'It was a horrific attack on a defenceless old

Capel St Mary Church.

lady in her home. The level of violence used can only be described as terrible.'

Joan Albert had been harassed by local youths in recent months. They had been knocking on her door and causing a general nuisance. She decided to install a security camera above her front door and she reported the matter to the police. One neighbour said that she was very security conscious and that her house was 'like Fort Knox'.

Suspicion fell on 25 year old Simon Hall from Ipswich. He utterly denied having broken into Joan's home and killed her. The old lady had been stabbed at least five times with a carving knife that had been taken from her kitchen.

Suspicion had fallen on Hall because he knew Mrs Albert; his mother did shopping for her and walked her dog. As far as Graham Parkins QC was concerned: 'He was in a position to know much about Joan Albert and formed his own view as to her worth, as he told a girlfriend that Joan came from a wealthy family.'

Hall faced the charge of murder at Norwich Crown Court. He told the court that he had been drinking on the night of the murder and that between 0400 and 0600 he had been walking

Norwich Crown Court where Steven Puacca and Simon Hall were tried.

around Ipswich to sober up before he drove home. He had an alibi for almost the entire evening and the early morning, apart from a period between 0530 and 0615.

What surprised the court was the fact that Hall, a well built, 6 feet tall man, had managed to squeeze himself through a 14 inch wide window. There were no fingerprints, footprints or DNA evidence to place Hall at the scene of the murder. However, fibres from a pair of black trousers that were found at the scene and in Hall's car and cupboard, the prosecution claimed, tied him to the murder. This was despite the fact of Hall and witnesses stating that he did not wear that type of trousers and that he was wearing blue ones on the night in question. Dr Heath was the pathologist in the case of Simon Hall and accusations about his conduct throw doubt on his evidence given in this case.

In his summing up Justice Rafferty cautioned the jury: 'There is no direct evidence to prove that Simon Hall murdered Joan Albert and that there is apparent circumstantial evidence and it's up to you how you wish to interpret it.'

It was alleged that as Lynne Hall was a close friend of Joan Albert she would instantly recognize Simon Hall and that is why he murdered her.

There is a considerable body of evidence that suggests that Simon Hall may not have murdered Joan Albert. The first suggestion is the lack of motive. Simon was in debt at the time, but not drastically so. This was put forward as one of the motives during the trial. Equally, if Simon Hall had burgled the house it was a fairly dangerous time of the morning to do it, when there would be paperboys and dog walkers about.

The opportunity for the murder is also interesting. Simon Hall's mother had a set of Joan Albert's keys. If he had intended to burgle the house, why did he not wait until his mother was out with Joan?

On the evening before the burglary and murder, Simon Hall had consumed a large amount of alcohol. When he returned home, the first person to see him was his mother and he displayed no signs of unusual behaviour.

Most serious are alleged errors that were made by the police and the pathologist. First, Lynne Hall was let into the house without protective clothing, along with two officers, also not wearing protective clothing. This occurred on 8 January 2002. This could easily have been the source of the contamination and the source of the fibres. The police spent a considerable amount of time trying to find the source of some pubic hair that had been found in Joan Albert's upstairs toilet. It transpired that the hair belonged to a police officer that had used the toilet.

Simon Hall was accused of having purchased the pair of trousers that were the supposed source of the fibres at a supermarket on the morning of the murder. However, he does not appear on any CCTV camera footage entering the supermarket, but does appear on CCTV using a cash machine outside the supermarket.

The most important consideration is that Simon Hall claims to have a significant alibi for the whole period. He arrived at the Old Rep public house at 2000 on 15 December. After a couple of drinks he and a friend headed for the Woolpack public house. He was well known to the landlord there. Simon and his friend drove from the Old Rep to the Woolpack. As he was now over the limit after drinking at the next pub Simon left his car keys with the landlord of the Woolpack. At around 2230 Simon and his friend headed back towards the Old Rep, arriving there at just before 2300. They then returned to the Woolpack again and around 0300 they went back for a lock-in at the Old Rep. By about 0430 Simon and another friend walked around Ipswich town to try and sober up. They headed back towards the Woolpack at around 0500, to try and get the car keys back from the landlord. Simon and his friend, Jamie Barker, headed home then. Jamie was dropped off at around 0530. Jamie would later say that he thought it could have been any time between 0530 and 0600. Simon then headed home to Capel St Mary. His mother was already up and he walked in at 0615.

The ornate village sign of Capel St Mary.

Later Simon would claim that he arrived home at around 0628, but could not be completely sure. This left a tiny gap in time, which the prosecution would later use to show that Simon Hall had the opportunity to carry out the burglary and murder.

As late as November 2006, with the Criminal Cases Review Commission looking at fifty cases involving Dr Heath, the Hall family had new hope about their son. He had been sentenced to life for the murder. The family said in November:

> *We feel strongly that Simon would not have been put at the scene even, and therefore not in the frame if Dr Heath had carried out the normal practice of visiting the crime scene immediately it was reported in the morning to ascertain the time of death instead of waiting to view Mrs Albert in the mortuary at 7.35 p.m., some ten hours later. We believe this man* [Dr Heath] *has made serious errors of judgement which has adversely affected cases with which he has been involved with profound effects of peoples lives, including our own.*

The investigations and re-examinations of the case is ongoing. But for Simon Hall the judge recommended that he would serve at least twelve years of his sentence before being considered for parole.

CHAPTER 20

Mother of Three

The Murder of Michelle Bettles, 31 March 2002

The body of 22 year old Michelle Bettles was discovered in a woodland area at Scarning, near Dereham on 31 March 2002. A man walking his dog in Podmore Lane, at 1015 on Sunday morning, found her body.

The police quickly established the fact that Michelle had been working as a prostitute in Norwich. She had been strangled. They were desperate to find out about her last movements and appealed for clients and other prostitutes to come forward. Several items of Michelle's property were missing, including her long, black leather coat and her handbag. Michelle was described as being around 5 feet 4 inches tall, slim, with long, dark, wavy hair. She had a mole on her nose and distinctive thick eyebrows.

When she was found, she was wearing a red tee shirt, a red wraparound skirt, beige tights and long, zipped, black boots.

Detective Inspector Howard Marriot said: 'At the present time there is no apparent link with any other murder or disappearance of women from this county or elsewhere.'

Chief Superintendent John Bainbridge, Central Area Commander, added:

> *We are aware that people may link this death to other incidents involving Norwich prostitutes. We understand that other prostitutes will therefore be concerned for their own welfare. Whilst officers working in Norwich will continue to deal with offences relating to prostitution, we will be focusing other police activities in relevant areas of the city in an attempt to ensure that women are not at risk. There is nothing to suggest from our enquiries that there is any threat to any other members of the public.*

A post mortem was carried out on Michelle on 1 April 2002. The Home Office Pathologist, Dr Michael Heath, confirmed that the cause of death was 'by manual strangulation'.

The police believed that Michelle had left her home, on the Dereham Road, to go to the red light district of Norwich. They had strong suspicions that the route she had taken had meant that she had walked along St Benedict's towards the city centre.

They were keen to trace a car close to the murder scene at Podmore, near Scarning. At around 2130 on the night of 30 March, an engine was heard 'racing'. Soon afterwards a Japanese-style 4 x 4 vehicle was seen driving away at speed in the direction of Dereham. Police had also found tyre prints on the verge of the road.

Detective Superintendent Chris Grant said:

We still believe that there are people who may have vital pieces of information and have not come forward. Did you see or hear anything unusual? A car engine being revved hard, details of any vehicles seen in the area?

Michelle's mother, who wished to remain anonymous, released a short statement via Norfolk police:

The public have heard that my daughter was a prostitute and a drug addict, but until other people changed her life, she was a normal, happy child who loved her family and we loved her. She did well at school and could have gone on to university.

The Dereham Road in Norwich.

Scarning Church.

She was a lovely child. I just want other parents to know what can happen to their children if they fall victim to the wrong influences. None of our children are safe from the evil people who deal in drugs and prostitution.

By July it seemed that the case was getting nowhere. Police had established that Michelle had made arrangements with two men on the night of 28 March.

The police were still appealing for help by November 2002. It was now clear that she had last been seen alive on the night of 28 March. Michelle was also confirmed as being a local woman. She had lived in Norwich for the majority of her life, but had connections in Dereham and Swaffham.

She had become a heroin addict and a prostitute to pay for her drugs. The police were convinced that there was a link, probably with the drugs, and her death. Detective Inspector David Ward said:

> *This is a tragic case involving the death of a young woman and mother of three. I have no doubt that someone knows who killed Michelle, or, at least, suspects a particular individual to have been involved in some way. We need that person to come forward and speak to us now.*

Ward was keen to track down any of Michelle's clients. He made an assurance that they would not be prosecuted but treated as valuable witnesses: 'I want to put their minds at rest, they will not face prosecution, they will be treated as witnesses. We need their help in solving this murder.'

On 26 March 2003, Norfolk police announced that they had made an arrest in the Norwich area related to the murder of Michelle Bettles. A 30 year old man was questioned by

The Rose, at the corner of Queens Road and City Road in Norwich.

police, but later released on bail. As far as future events were concerned, this enquiry seemed to have led nowhere.

By August 2003 the enquiry had begun to grind to a halt and the number of officers on the enquiry had been scaled down. Rumours abounded regarding the potential killer of Michelle Bettles. Some believe that there was a link between Michelle's death and the murder of three other Norwich prostitutes in the period of a decade. Natalie Pearman, Kelly Pratt and Hayley Curtis. There were also rumours that the murderer was a 30 year old man from the Long Stratton area.

Detective Chief Superintendent Chris Grant was clearly unsure as to whether there was a connection between the four murders:

> *I am very aware of the history of Norwich involving the murder and/or disappearance of women and I am keeping very much an open mind. I have nothing at the moment to suggest that these incidents are in any way connected – nor can I exclude that they might be connected.*

In January 2002 the body of Hayley Curtis, a Norwich prostitute, was found in a shallow grave in Hampshire. In June 2000, Kelly Pratt, another prostitute, had vanished and is presumed dead. In 1992 a client strangled Natalie Pearman and her body was dumped five miles away.

The police had launched a study, code named Operation Enigma. They looked at seventy-two murders of young women and found that fourteen of them bore the same hallmark, which suggested that it could be the work of a serial killer. Another prostitute, this time working in the red light district near Portman Road in Ipswich, mother of two, Mandy Duncan (26), had vanished without trace in July 1993.

The inquest finally took place in October 2003, ruling that Michelle had been unlawfully killed. The Coroner, William Armstrong, hoped that the verdict would allow Michelle's parents to move on. Michelle's father, John, said:

> *It's just a chapter that's closed. Obviously there's other chapters still open. I believe that one day somebody is going to be punished and hopefully I'll be there to see it. People who say forgive – no way.*

Her mother, still not wishing to be named, said:

The only thing that's going to stop my grief is if they catch her killer – that's basically all it is.

John Bettles added:

At some point the police are going to knock on their door and they're going to be sat down with their wife and kids having their tea. I'm carrying on fighting. If this stops one other family going through the pain we've been through then it's worth it. I'm determined not to see this vanish into the archives.

At its height, Norfolk police had dedicated thirty-five officers to the murder enquiry. The enquiry itself had lasted over eighteen months and they had taken 1,700 witness statements. This did not dissuade John Bettles from claiming that because of what Michelle did for a living it made the case a low priority:

If she'd been a shopkeeper or a sales assistant or someone with a normal life, the case would have got the coverage it deserves – and it does deserve it because there are three kids out there with no one to call mum.

The man that had been arrested just after 0600 on 26 March 2003 had initially denied ever meeting Michelle. Finally, however, he admitted that he had picked her up and driven her home and then called a taxi for her to be driven back to Norwich. DNA showed conclusively that he had been with Michelle two days before her death. He had used prostitutes before. In the end he was released without charge, leaving the police to consider their own theories about his involvement.

Forensic tests showed that Michelle's body had been stored overnight before being dumped, leading police to look at plants retrieved forensically. Again they focused on a suspect, a farmer, whose happy marriage and flourishing business had been destroyed by drink. All enquiries led to frustration and failure. Even in 2005, police were still requesting anything that anyone could remember about the Easter weekend when the Queen Mother had also died.

CHAPTER 21

Conned

The Death of Thelma Avis, 4 July 2003

At 1730 on the afternoon of Friday, 4 July 2003, 90 year old Thelma Avis made her way to the front door, using her walking frame. Standing outside was a white male, aged between 20 and 30 years old, around 5 feet 8 inches tall, slim with short, dark brown, straight hair. He was clean-shaven and had a sallow complexion and was wearing a long-sleeved, navy top with blue jeans and grey trainers. Beyond him Thelma could see a red Escort type van. The man claimed to be from the gas board and that he was investigating a leak. He then walked, uninvited, into Thelma's Barn Hall Avenue home in Colchester, Essex, refusing to show any identification.

After about twenty-five minutes inside the house Thelma telephoned one of her sons, who lived close by. At that point the man left the house and later £1,000 of cash was discovered to be missing.

When the police arrived both of Thelma's sons were with her. She seemed well enough and was able to give a good description of the man. The police left Thelma and the family at 2030 in the evening, but at 2120 an ambulance was called because Thelma had collapsed. The police were informed at 2200 that Thelma had died.

A post mortem would later reveal that although Thelma had heart disease, the trauma of the burglary had been the direct cause of her death.

The police believed that the man that entered the semi-detached house had an accomplice with him. They also believed that they were a team, possibly of two or three that had carried out similar offences in the area. Thelma had been sure that the man that had spoken to her and entered her home had a Colchester accent. The police were piecing together information of the descriptions of two other men. The first was just 5 feet tall, in his early twenties, tanned with short hair and an Irish accent. The other was a similar age, seven inches taller, with medium build, also tanned and he had a beige coloured baseball cap.

Within a few days three men were arrested on suspicion of burglary and murder. In fact one was a 17 year old from Colchester, another a 19 year old from Colchester and the third a 19 year old from Cornwall. They were quickly eliminated from the enquiry. Another three men were arrested much later, in February 2004; two were aged 18, and one aged 19 and they were all from the Colchester area. They were eventually released without charge.

In linking the burglary to the death of Thelma, the police were not just looking for burglars, but murderers, as Detective Superintendent Kevin Macey said:

Had the burglary not taken place there is every likelihood that Mrs Avis would be alive today. For that reason the case is being treated as a murder enquiry. Associates of the bogus caller may know about the theft but are probably unaware of the tragic aftermath and may now want to come forward.

Detective Superintendent Macey described the crime as 'callous and despicable'. He went on to say:

I am convinced that the shock and trauma of this incident has led to the death of an elderly woman who was not in the best of health.

Thelma's two sons, Neil and John, made appeals at a press conference:

Our mother was always there for us and those people have deprived us of a loving, caring mother who was housebound, elderly and frail. I am at a loss for words. These people have thoughts only for themselves and not for the misery they have left behind. They might be criminals, but they too may have elderly relatives. They should put themselves in our place.

Shortly after the crime, staff at Old Heath Post Office believed that one of the men tried to pass Thelma's stolen money through the shop. Just two hours after the robbery a man aged between 20 and 30 came into the store. He wanted to change money and was acting suspiciously. When he left the store he got into a red Renault car that had three other men inside it. The Old Heath Post Office put up a £500 reward. Thelma had been a regular customer and one of her sons collected her paper and pension for her from the store. The sub-postmaster, Riaz Maghoo, said:

> *I feel deeply sorry for Mr Avis. He is a loyal customer and what has happened is disgusting. We are going to try and help as much as we can.*

A week after the death of Thelma, police were stopping vehicles in Barn Hall Avenue. It was a major operation for the Colchester police. The road checks took place between 1400 and 1800, and 600 vehicles were subjected to them. The police were firmly of the opinion that this was a distraction burglary and that indeed one of the man's accomplices had actually been responsible for stealing the money from Thelma's house.

Just a few days after the death of Thelma another incident took place, this time in Sargeants Close in Colchester. Again a man presented himself as a representative of the gas board, investigating a leak. The incident took place at 1400 in the afternoon but this time there were two men. One had dark brown, cropped hair, with a tanned complexion and was in his mid-thirties. The other was nearly 6 feet tall with longer hair but was around the same age. The house targeted was only a quarter of a mile from Thelma's home. This time, however, the bogus callers were out of luck, as when they refused to show any identification the woman slammed the door in their face and called the police. The men made off in a small, white van.

There were more distraction burglaries in the area, again in July 2003. A con woman this time tricked an 86 year old woman in Wellesley Road, Clacton out of a large amount of cash. She presented herself at the door, saying that she would sort out the pensioner's garden. When she left she had taken a large amount of the woman's money.

Bogus callers and distraction burglaries seemed to be showing all the signs of being an epidemic in Essex. Two years after Thelma's death the police admitted that hundreds of pensioners each year were suffering the same tragic fate. In April 2005 alone seventy-six elderly people were conned, but the average in Essex is forty per month.

Braintree is at the top of the bogus caller rankings. In a police statement in May 2005, Detective Sergeant Trevor Garrard admitted that the bogus caller crimes could mean that another tragedy, such as the one suffered by the Avis family, was inevitable.

The police had launched Operation Grisly Bear in an attempt to target the conmen. In 2005 they launched Operation Splash, another initiative which helped to raise the detection rates from just 4 per cent to 25 per cent.

Thelma's case is still open. As Detective Chief Superintendent Macey said in July 2005, two years after Thelma's death: 'It's a scar on my reputation.'

He was convinced that one day he would find the killers and was still in charge of the hunt to bring them to justice:

> *We will never give up. It is two years on and we're still looking at it. Other cases have diverted our attention at times, but it is not forgotten.*

CHAPTER 22

An Essex Trio

The murders of Martin Broom (22 July 1989), John Marshall (May 1996) and 'Joe' Shipton (March 2006)

These three unconnected Essex murders illustrate the problems faced by the police in their investigations, particularly when there appears to be no motive for the murder.

On 2 July 1989 Martin Broom, aged 29, was found murdered in his home at Sussex Close, Boreham near Chelmsford. It would have been a perfectly ordinary Saturday morning, but the police discovered that Broom had been beaten to death as he lay in bed. The weapon was a small hammer belonging to Broom and it was recovered at the scene of the murder. A pair of bloodstained pipe wrenches that were manufactured in India were also recovered near the scene. There was

Sussex Close, Boreham near Chelmsford.

no sign of a forced entry, but the house had been ransacked, although nothing appeared to have been taken.

Broom ran his own business, Cresta Forklift Services. He was a keen sub-aqua diver, one of the many sports he was involved with. In fact he had been at the Chelmsford Sub-Aqua Club at the Riverside Centre in Chelmsford only the night before.

There was some speculation in national newspapers that Broom had been tortured and murdered on account of the fact that someone believed he knew where there was some sunken treasure. It was put forward that he intended to dive for the treasure and that whoever killed him wanted to know the details of his secret. His fellow divers dismissed this as being nonsense.

There had been several arrests during the course of the enquiries, but no one was ever charged. There had been the potential to find innumerable witnesses for that weekend. There was an acid house party going on in the area and it was the view of the police that someone had definitely seen something.

All the police had to go on was the sighting of a red Vauxhall

The Riverside Ice and Leisure Centre, Chelmsford.

Astra, which had been seen regularly visiting Broom's home in Sussex Close. The occupants of the car were both blonde, one male seen with silver wrap around glasses. The only description of the woman was that she was slim.

Another sighting was that of an 18 to 25 year old woman with dark, feathery cut hair. She had been seen at Broom's address, having driven there in a green/brown Mini estate. There was some speculation that this woman may actually have been a man dressed as a woman.

The second perplexing murder has parallels with the Rettenden killings, which were, in turn, possibly connected to the Ronald Fuller murder. This time the victim was John Marshall. He was nearly 35 and he had two daughters then aged 13 and 3 and a son aged 6. The last time he was seen was 15 May 1996, three days short of his thirty-fifth birthday.

As he drove away from his home in Billericay at 1000 on 15 May he took with him presents that his children had bought him for his birthday. He was off to finalize a business deal in Kent and was driving a black Range Rover. The police believe that he crossed the Thames via the Queen Elizabeth II Bridge into Kent at about 1200 on the same day. But he failed to keep his appointments and he did not return home.

Marshall's wife, Toni, usually received several calls from her husband during the day. By the evening, without word, she contacted the police and reported him missing. It took the police until 22 May to find the car. It had been abandoned at Round Hill, Sydenham in south London. The police made enquiries about the vehicle and it appeared that it was left there early in the morning the day following Marshall's disappearance.

Inside the unlocked boot of the car the police made a gruesome discovery. Hidden in piles of straw in the boot was John Marshall's body. He had been shot twice in the head and twice in the chest. It bore the hallmarks of an execution. The only thing that the police were sure about with regard to the weapon was that it was not a shotgun.

The keys to the Range Rover were missing, as was a grey sports bag, an 18-carat gold watch and a pair of mobile phones. Oddly, if robbery had been the motive, there was still £5,000 in cash in the vehicle that Marshall had taken with him the morning he left home to complete the business deal.

Marshall was a devoted family man and the police could find no clear links between him and criminals or illegal activities. They were at a loss to understand why this hitherto respectable car dealer had been assassinated in such a way.

Just like the other two men, the third victim of an unsolved murder was an ordinary, unassuming individual. Michael Shipton was aged 61. He was better known as Joe Shipton and he lived on his own in The Plashets, Sheering village, which is close to Harlow.

According to the senior investigating officer, Detective Superintendent Simon Dinsdale:

> *Joe was murdered some time between the afternoon of Friday 24 March and the morning of Saturday 25 March. He was killed in a cowardly fashion while in the sanctuary of his own home. Hopefully, this enhanced reward will persuade anyone with information as to what happened inside Joe's house to contact us.*

Dinsdale was referring to a £5,000 reward for information leading to the arrest and prosecution of the murderer of Joe Shipton. His neighbours described Joe as a 'very friendly, nice guy'.

The Essex ambulance service had been called at 0938 on Saturday, 25 March. The ambulance crew found the body of Joe Shipton and, concerned about the cause of his death, immediately contacted the police. The crew remained on the scene for an hour and a half while they gave statements to the police.

It transpired that Joe's body was found at the bottom of the stairs of his home. The post mortem showed that he had died from head injuries caused by a heavy weapon, such as a baseball bat.

The murder enquiry was launched five days after the discovery of the body, straight after the confirmation of the post mortem results. At that stage Dinsdale said:

> *Joe was well known in the community. He travelled everywhere on his bicycle and undertook odd jobs here and there. We need to build up a picture of his life and background from where he was last seen and by whom to what work he had been doing and where he had been.*

Just like the Martin Broom case there was no sign of a forced entry to the house. This led the police to assume that Joe had known his attacker. One of Joe's neighbours said:

> *He was a nice guy. I always found him very friendly and*

everyone else would say the same thing. I am extremely sad to think that something like that could happen here. It's a terrible time. Our little village has been shattered. You live in a backwater and you don't think it could happen.

In fact Joe Shipton had lived in the same house for over thirty years. Initially the house had belonged to his parents.

Joe was a quiet man and a regular at the pub, The Cock, as landlord Bill Bedford recalled:

He was an unassuming sort of bloke who didn't have any enemies and will probably have gone out of his way not to upset people. He should have been here drinking with us on Sunday but now there's a gap in our circle of friends. It's very sad.

One man, Albert Mason, had known Joe for twenty-four years and he was understandably shocked by the death of his close friend:

We just thought he had died of natural causes, a heart attack or something like that. Then all of a sudden it changed to murder.

At the time of writing, nearly a year after the murder of Joe Shipton, the case remains unsolved, as do the cases of Martin Broom and John Marshall.

Index